David Suzuki

and Kathy Vanderlinden

Great projects, experiments, and games for a greener earth

ECO-FUN

David Suzuki Foundation

GREYSTONE BOOKS
Douglas & McIntyre Publishing Group
Vancouver/Toronto/New York

Greystone Books
A division of Douglas & McIntyre Ltd.
2323 Quebec Street, Suite 201
Vancouver, British Columbia V5T 4S7
www.greystonebooks.com

David Suzuki Foundation
219-2211 West 4th Avenue
Vancouver, British Columbia V6K 4S2

Canadian Cataloguing in Publication Data

Suzuki, David, 1936–
    Eco-fun

    Copublished by: David Suzuki Foundation
    Includes index.
    ISBN 1-55054-823-9

    1. Environmental sciences—Juvenile literature. 2. Ecology—Juvenile
literature. I. Vanderlinden, Kathy. II. David Suzuki Foundation. III. Title.
GE115.S89 2001   j577   C00-911469-6

Library of Congress Cataloging-in-Publication data is available.

Editing by Nancy Flight
Text design by Warren Clark
Cover design by Peter Cocking
Cover photograph of David Suzuki by Chick Rice
Cover photograph of experiment by Raeff Miles
Illustrations by Jane Kurisu

Printed and bound in Canada by Friesens

The publisher gratefully acknowledges the support of the Canada Council
for the Arts and of the British Columbia Ministry of Tourism, Small Business
and Culture. The publisher also acknowledges the financial support of the
Government of Canada through the Book Publishing Industry Development
Program (BPIDP) for its publishing activities.

Greystone Books is committed to reducing the consumption of old-growth
forests in the books it publishes. This book is one step toward that goal. It
is printed on acid-free paper that is 100% ancient-forest-free, and it has
been processed chlorine free.

Contents

A Message from David Suzuki

When I was a boy, I had a magic place I could always go to and discover something new and wonderful. It was a swamp I could easily reach by bicycle. One day I found an injured crow there and watched in amazement as its fellow crows circled and cawed overhead trying to help. I spotted skunks, raccoons, herons, and once a fox at that boggy place. Many times I came home dripping wet and triumphant with frog or salamander eggs, minnows, crayfish, and turtles for my aquarium.

That swamp fueled my imagination, revealed a world of unimaginable beauty and variety, and gave me a lifelong passion for nature. It's not an accident that I ended up as a biologist studying genetics in insects. And most researchers I have met also became scientists because as children they were enchanted by some part of nature, such as stars, butterflies, or flowers.

These days, more and more of us live in big cities. The ponds, woods, bogs, ditches, and creeks that I spent so much of my childhood exploring have become harder to find or reach. It's easier to surf the Net, play video games, or cruise the mall. We are surrounded by human beings and all our spectacular inventions, like computers, VCRs, cars, and planes. It's easy to forget that we are biological beings, and just like our pet dogs or cats and our garden flowers or carrots we need clean air, clean water, clean food, and clean energy to be healthy.

Think about everything in your home, your school, or your parents' workplace—where did computer parts, electricity, and your clothes and books come from? Plastic, glass, energy, meat, vegetables—everything comes from the Earth. Earth is the source of all we use, including everything in our bodies—muscle, blood, bone, and hair. It's no wonder that Native people all over the world refer to the Earth as our mother.

The best way to learn about the world around us is to experience it. We will work to protect those things we love, and we learn to love those things we have made a connection with. This book contains activities that will help you see and experience the world in a different way, bring you into contact with nature, and remind you that you are a child of the Earth.

Introduction

This book is called *Eco-Fun*. "Eco" is short for "ecology," and "fun"—you know what that is. The activities you're about to have fun with have to do with ecology—the relationship of living things to each other and to everything in their surroundings, or homes. ("Eco" comes from a Greek word meaning "house.")

The idea that things are connected to each other is important. Scientists have found that what keeps the Earth alive and healthy is everything in it working in harmony with everything else. That means the air, water, earth or soil, energy from the sun, and Earth's great family of plants and animals must work together as a team.

What does that have to do with you? Well, you're an animal—a human animal—so you're part of the team. To live, you need clean air to breathe, fresh water to drink, fertile earth in which to grow food, and the sun's fire to fuel spaceship Earth. And you need biodiversity—millions of different kinds of plants and animals living in many different kinds of habitats.

You probably think of all those things as outside you. But strange as it seems, they are inside you too. You breathe in air, filter it through your body, and breathe out carbon dioxide, a gas that plants take in. You drink water and then pass it back to the environment in body wastes such as sweat. You eat food that is grown in the earth, watered by rain, and given energy by the sun. And all those plants and animals clean the air, make the soil fertile, and take in the sun's energy and pass it on to you. You have water, air, and energy in every cell of your body.

So you see how important it is for us humans to do our bit to keep the Earth healthy. Unfortunately, we haven't been doing a very good job of it lately. We've built a world of space shuttles and skyscrapers and computers that is exciting but that has seriously harmed the natural world. We need to learn how to balance our desire for progress and possessions with our need for a healthy Earth so that it will be around for your great-grandchildren and their children to enjoy.

Get to know the marvelous natural world that is our home. As you explore it through the activities in this book, you'll be working with air, water, soil, energy, plants, and animals. Some activities help you understand what these elements are, what they do, or how they are connected to you. Some show how they are being damaged and what can be done about that. Some give you ideas for helping to make the Earth a better place.

A few reminders. Read each activity before you start so that you won't have any nasty surprises when you're halfway through. Often you can improvise if you don't have an item you need—for example, you can make a funnel by rolling thick paper into a cone shape. Raid the recycling box for containers. Ask for help when you need it, and get your friends involved. And most of all, have fun!

Be Safe and Sound

Protect yourself

Some of the activities in this book include Safety Tips to help you avoid accidents, such as cutting your finger or setting the house on fire. Here's a summary to keep in mind as you work through the book:

∗ Always read over an activity before starting so that you know exactly what you'll be doing. When you do the activity, pay close attention as you follow each step. You'll get more out of the project that way, too.

∗ Ask an adult to help you when you're working with matches, a stove, electrical appliances, knives, a drill, or a hammer and nails.

∗ When you're outdoors, never look directly at the sun. That can damage your eyes.

∗ Wear safety goggles when you are smashing rocks with a hammer or doing anything else that might endanger your eyes.

∗ Unless the activity invites you to eat or taste something, don't.

∗ It's a good idea to wear gardening or rubber gloves when handling soil. It might have harmful bacteria in it.

∗ Wash your hands after finishing an activity.

Protect the natural world

∗ Treat all natural things—animals, plants, soil, and water—with care and respect.

∗ Keep any animals you're working with safe. Handle them gently and be sure that they have food, water, and air. When you're finished, put them back where you found them.

∗ Get permission before you collect any plants. Be careful not to disturb the area around them.

∗ Whenever you are doing an activity outdoors, create as little disturbance to the area as possible.

∗ Whenever possible, recycle or reuse materials—such as paper and water— that you have used in your activity.

1 A Breath of Fresh Air

You can't see it and you can't grab hold of it, but you need air every second of your life. It's all around you and inside you, being breathed in and breathed out. Air is inside every animal and plant in the world. And we all exchange the air with each other.

Let's say you're sitting with your dog on the floor. You and Rex are breathing the same air. You breathe atoms (invisible bits) of air out, and Rex breathes some of those same atoms in. Then he breathes atoms out, and you . . . Well, you get the idea. It gives new meaning to the phrase "man's best friend."

So what is air? Air is a gas (invisible floaty stuff that doesn't have shape) made up of about 78 percent nitrogen, 21 percent oxygen, and 1 percent other gases. Oxygen is the most important gas for us animals, because it is burned in our bodies, where it does essential work, such as keeping our brains alert.

Another gas we always have inside us is carbon dioxide. We create it ourselves. When our bodies digest food or build muscles, for example, carbon dioxide is produced as a by-product. We don't need it, so we breathe most of it out into the air.

And here's the really great part. Plants do just the opposite—they take in carbon dioxide and give off oxygen. So plants and animals have a system of give-and-take going that helps them both. Plants provide much of the oxygen in the air. Half a

hectare (1 acre) of trees can release 1900 kilograms (4200 pounds) of oxygen into the air in a year.

Trees also help clean the air by soaking up pollutants such as sulfur dioxide and ozone. (We need ozone high up to protect us from the sun's ultraviolet rays, but at ground level it is damaging to our cells). But sometimes our air gets so polluted that trees and other plants can't clean it up. Instead, the pollution damages or kills them.

Air pollution comes from factories, homes, cars, and trucks. The dangerous chemicals that they send into the air fall on plants, water, and soil and are breathed in by people and all the other animals in the area.

Governments and companies can do a lot to help clean up our air. For example, automobile manufacturers have built a new kind of car that runs on a combination of gas and electric power. These "hybrid" cars release fewer polluting chemicals than regular cars do.

The combined efforts of individuals, families, and communities can make a big difference, too. The following activities will give you some ideas.

Something in the Air

You can't see air, but it does exist. These two experiments show how real air is.

What you need

- A large clear glass or plastic bowl
- ½ sheet of newspaper
- A clear juice glass
- A piece of stiff, light cardboard about 12 cm (5 inches) square

What to do

A GLASS OF AIR

1. Do this experiment in a large sink. Put the bowl in the sink and fill it with water.

2. Crumple the newspaper and wedge it into the bottom of the glass. Hold the glass upside down and push it straight down to the bottom of the bowl. (Make sure the water is deep enough to cover the glass.) Pull the glass straight back out. Did the paper get wet? Try submerging the glass right side up. Now what happens?

MAGIC CARDBOARD

1. Do this part over the sink, too. Empty the glass and then fill it half full of water.

2. Wet the rim with your finger and put the cardboard on top.

3. Press the cardboard firmly against the rim so that no air gets in. Still pressing the cardboard with one hand, turn the glass upside down with the other hand. Now carefully let go of the cardboard. Did the trick work the first time? What would happen if you turned the glass sideways before letting go?

What's going on?

In "A Glass of Air," water didn't fill the glass because the glass was already full of something that couldn't get out—air. But when you put the glass into the water right side up, air wasn't trapped in an enclosed space, so water rushed in. In "Magic Cardboard," the water stayed in the glass because the pressure of the air in the room pushing against the cardboard was stronger than the pressure of the water against the cardboard.

A Weighty Matter

Air has not only substance (it's a "thing") and pressure but also mass. Try weighing some air.

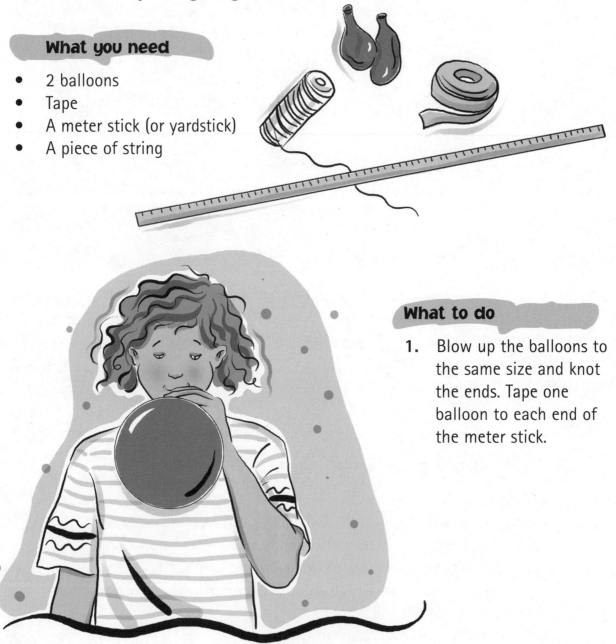

What you need

- 2 balloons
- Tape
- A meter stick (or yardstick)
- A piece of string

What to do

1. Blow up the balloons to the same size and knot the ends. Tape one balloon to each end of the meter stick.

2. Tie one end of the string around the middle of the stick. Tape the other end to the edge of a ledge or table so that the stick hangs level like a mobile. If the balloons don't balance, move the string on the meter stick until they do. You now have a scale with equal weights on either end.

3. Now prick one of the balloons. What happens? Why?

What's going on?

The full balloon goes down because it has air in it, making it weigh more than the punctured balloon. The weight of air depends a lot on how warm it is. Warm air is lighter than cool air. Many weather events, such as clouds forming or breaking up, are caused by warm air rising or cool air falling.

Watch Plants Make Oxygen

We all need to breathe in oxygen every second of our lives. Where does oxygen come from? Plants "breathe" it out through their leaves. You can see that happen in this experiment. Set up your apparatus in the kitchen sink—this one can get messy.

What you need

- A large clear glass or plastic bowl
- A medium-sized clear plastic container
- Water plants (for example, pond weed from a pond or from a store that sells aquarium supplies)

What to do

1. In a large sink, fill the bowl with water.

2. Put the plastic container in the bowl sideways and let it fill up with water. Scrunch the container down so that the entire mouth is under water and no air can get in.

3. Keeping the mouth completely under water, turn the container upside down in the bowl.

4. Carefully ease the water plants under the container. Don't let any of the water get out.

5. If necessary, tip a little water out of the bowl so that you can carry it without spilling. Lift it out of the sink and place it in a sunny spot. Leave it for a few hours. What happens?

6. Leave the bowl a little longer. Now what do you see?

What's going on?

The first thing you should see is streams of oxygen bubbles rising in the plastic container. Like all green plants, your water plants are making oxygen as part of photosynthesis (see "That Good Old Green Stuff" on page 26). After you have left the bowl a little longer, you will see a little air space forming at the top of the container. The oxygen has pushed out some of the water.

💡 More ideas . . .

- Mix a few drops of food coloring in the bowl when you fill it—you'll see the water better.

- Plants photosynthesize faster in a bright light. Shine a lamp onto your water plants and watch things speed up.

Dirty-Air Detectors

Just as you can't see air, you often can't see the pollution in it. How clean is the air you're breathing?

What you need

- Several plastic drinking glasses, well washed and dried
- Petroleum jelly
- A magnifying glass
- A notebook and pen or pencil
- The same number of large empty tin cans as drinking glasses, tops and bottoms removed
- Masking tape

What to do

1. Decide where you want to test for air pollution. Choose a variety of sites, including some you think are pretty clean (for example, your room, your yard, a park), some you think are dirty (near a highway), and some in between (a downtown street).

2. Smear the outside of one of the glasses with petroleum jelly and examine it with your magnifying glass. In your notebook, write down what you see. You need to know what a clean glass looks like so that you can compare your findings with it later.

3. Put the glass at your first test spot. Label it with a piece of masking tape stuck to the inside. Cover the glass with a can. The can will keep out most dust from the ground that would confuse the results. Now you have your first detector.

4. Make the rest of your detectors and put them at your test sites. Be sure to label each detector with the name of the site. Try to find spots where they'll be protected from rain. (Rain could wash away the evidence.)

5. Check the detectors every day for a week and record any changes in your notebook.

6. Collect the detectors at the end of the week and examine them carefully with your magnifying glass. Do you see much difference between the glasses? Have you caught any strange-looking particles, or specks? Are there any surprises?

7. Here's a rough pollution guide: Mark a 0.5-cm (1/4-inch) square on each collector and count the number of particles you see. If there are around 15, the site is probably fairly clean. But if there are 100 or more, try not to breathe too deeply in that area!

More ideas . . .

For a permanent record, collect 2 or 3 leaves from each test site in labeled plastic bags. At home, press a strip of clear tape against each leaf on both the top and underneath sides. Any particles will stick to the tape. Remove the pieces of tape, put them in your notebook, and label them with the site names. Do you notice any differences between these results and those from the glass detectors?

BACKYARD   HIGHWAY

PARK

Summer Coolers

On a hot day it's always cooler under a tree. The leafy branches shade you from the sun, but that's not all. Plants cool the air around them through transpiration. Here's how it works.

What you need

- A small bush or tree
- A small plastic bag
- A pebble
- A twist tie
- A measuring cup
- Measuring spoons

What to do

1. Look for a healthy bush or tree. Find a leafy stem at the end of a branch.

2. Blow into your bag to make sure it doesn't have any holes in it. (It should inflate like a balloon.) Put the pebble into the bag and fit the bag around the leaves and stem.

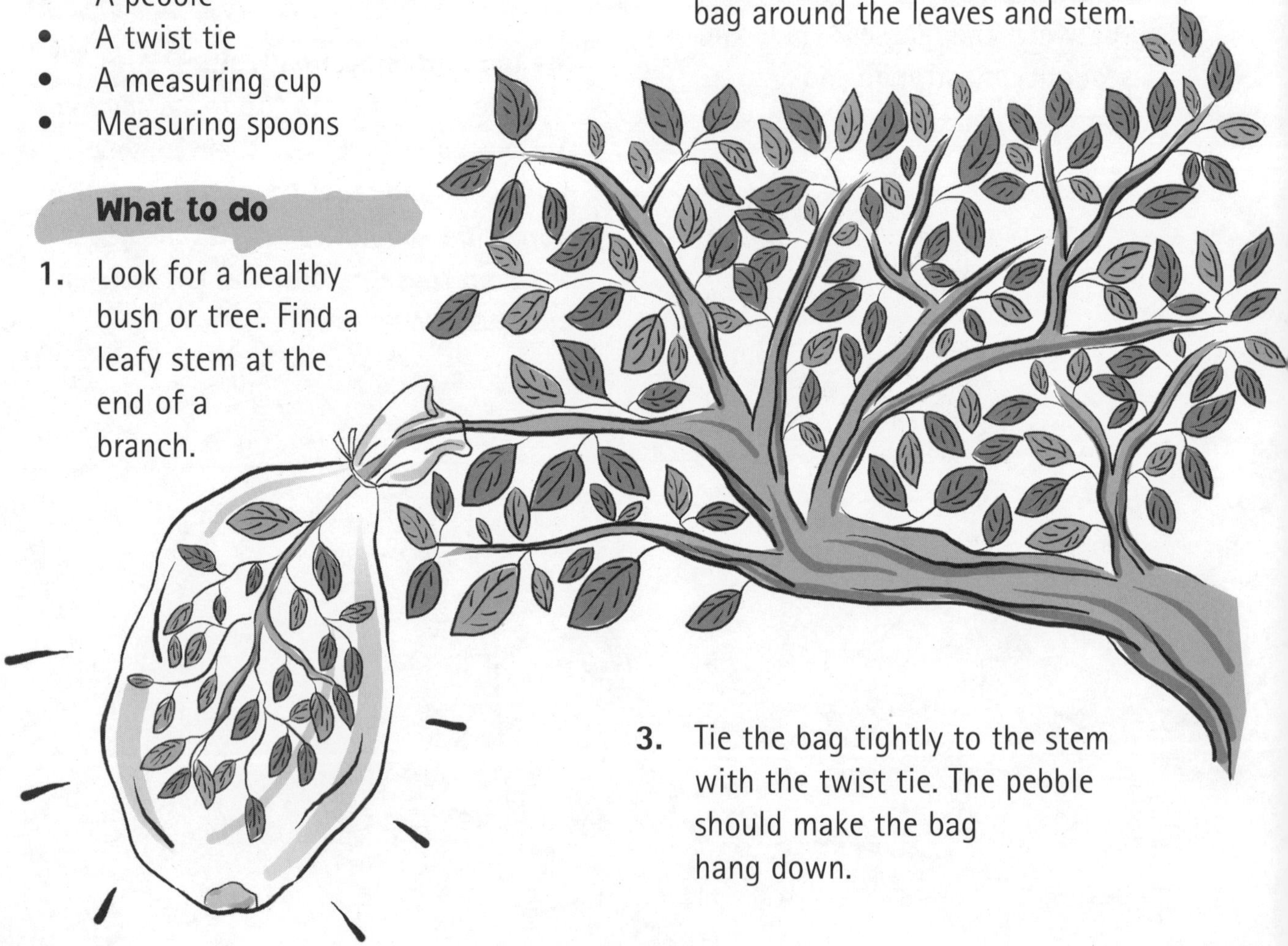

3. Tie the bag tightly to the stem with the twist tie. The pebble should make the bag hang down.

4. Check the bag 24 hours later. It will have water in it. Remove the bag and carefully pour the water into the measuring cup. If there is too little water to measure by cup, use the spoons.

5. Now do the math: Divide the amount of water by the number of leaves on the stem. That will give you the amount of water that each leaf transpired (gave off). For example, let's say you have 50 mL (3 tablespoons) of water and 5 leaves. That means that each leaf has given off 10 mL (about 2 teaspoons) of water (50 mL ÷ 5 leaves = 10 mL). Now count the number of leaves on the bush or tree. Multiply that number by the amount of water given off by one leaf to get the amount the whole bush transpired in a day. Are you impressed?

What's going on?

Just as we perspire through pores in our skin, leaves transpire through tiny openings called stomata. In this process, water in the leaves changes to water vapor (a gas). This change uses up heat energy in the air—in other words, it cools the air. A large tree can send many liters of water vapor into the air on a hot day. A forest can send so much that it affects climate and rainfall in that area.

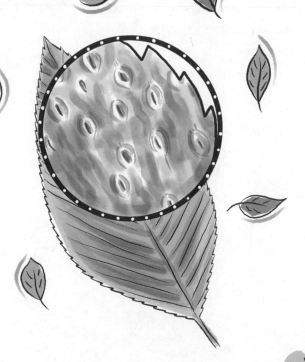

Pick a Coin, Any Coin

This activity shows you some neat things about the properties of air and water. But mostly it shows you how to tease and mystify your friends! Be sure to rehearse this trick before you perform it.

What you need

- A shallow clear or white dish
- A large, clear drinking glass
- Cooking oil
- A small, thin coin (for example, a dime)
- Food coloring
- Water
- A birthday candle
- A small candleholder (for example, a spice-bottle cap with large sprinkle holes)
- Matches

What to do

1. First, set the stage. Rub the dish and the rim of the glass very lightly with oil. Put the coin in the dish near one side.

2. Color about a cupful of water so that you'll be able to see it better. Slowly pour just enough into the dish to barely cover the coin. This is important! If you put in too much water, the trick won't work.

3. Next, you need an audience. A few friends and your dog will do.

Challenge your friends to remove the coin from the dish without getting their fingers wet and without using an instrument to fish it out of the water. They also can't pour off the water or move the dish in any way.

4. When everyone has given up, tell them you will remove the coin using only your magic candle, match, and glass.

What's going on?

Fire needs oxygen to burn. When the candle flame has used up nearly all the oxygen from the air inside the glass, it goes out. By burning the oxygen, the flame partly emptied the glass of air—in other words, it created a partial vacuum in the glass. Since air flows in to fill any vacuum, the pressure of the air outside forced air into the glass, pulling the water along with it.

SAFETY TIP
BE SURE YOU HAVE PERMISSION TO USE MATCHES, OR HAVE AN ADULT STANDING BY.

5. Put the candle in the candleholder and place it in the dish as far from the coin as possible. Light the candle and put the glass over it

6. When the candle goes out, the water will be drawn up into the glass. Now you can simply pick up the coin from the dry dish.

💡 More ideas . . .

Add the cardboard trick from "Something in the Air" to your Magic Air Show. Challenge your friends to hold a glass of water upside down without spilling a drop.

That Good Old Green Stuff

Plants give off oxygen as a waste product of their main job, which is to make food. These experiments take a look at that marvelous process, called photosynthesis. If you don't have a "green thumb" now, you might have one after this activity.

What you need

- 4 or 5 fresh leaves of different kinds
- Saucers or other containers
- Rubbing alcohol
- Cardboard
- Scissors
- Paper clips
- Petroleum jelly

What to do

1. Put all but one of the leaves into separate containers. Cover each leaf with alcohol. After a few hours, check your containers. What has happened?

2. Carefully tear the last leaf across. Look closely along the tear. On the underneath side you'll see a thin, transparent layer. If you could look at it under a microscope, you would see tiny holes called stomata, the plant's breathing holes (see page 23).

3. Cut some small shapes out of cardboard. You might want to cut out your initials. Find a bush or tree outside with fresh green leaves. Attach your shapes to several leaves with the paper clips. The shapes should cover just part of the leaf. Take the patches off in about a week and check the leaves. What do you see?

4. At the same time as you're patching your leaves, choose another leaf for a different treatment. Coat the leaf with a layer of petroleum jelly. Can light still get through? Check your leaf after a few days. What has happened? Compare this leaf with the patched leaves. What are the differences?

What's going on?

Food is made by the leaves. They use energy from the sun, carbon dioxide from the air, water and nutrients from the soil, and their own green coloring, called chlorophyll. In step 1, the alcohol turned green because it dissolved some chlorophyll in the leaves. In step 3, the cardboard stopped sunlight from getting to part of the leaf, so photosynthesis couldn't take place. In step 4, the transparent jelly let light get through, but it blocked the stomata, so the leaf couldn't breathe.

Seeing the Heat

The temperature of the air makes a big difference to how it behaves. Try these activities and you'll see some hot action.

BALLOON EXPANSE

What you need

- A small plastic bottle
- A balloon

What to do

1. Put the bottle in the refrigerator to cool it.

2. Stretch the neck of the balloon over the top of the bottle.

3. Run some hot water in a sink or dishpan. Put the bottle in the water and hold it in place. What happens? Why?

4. Put the bottle and balloon back in the refrigerator for about 5 minutes. Now what happens?

SPIRAL DANCE

What you need

- A pencil
- A piece of thick paper (for example, a magazine cover)
- Scissors
- A piece of thin string about 30 cm (12 inches) long

What to do

1. Draw a spiral about 15 cm (6 inches) across on your paper (see the picture). Cut it out along the circular lines.

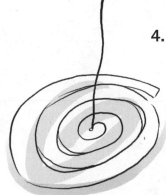

2. Use the scissors to poke a small hole in the center of the spiral. Knot one end of the string. Push the other end through the hole from underneath and pull it through to the knot.

3. Hold your spiral over a heater, radiator, or hot light bulb. What happens?

SAFETY TIP
DON'T TEST THE SPIRAL OVER HOT STOVES, FIREPLACES, CANDLES, OR OTHER FLAMES, SINCE THE PAPER COULD CATCH FIRE.

4. Test other spots in your home for hot air currents. Where do you find rising warm air?

What's going on?

When air heats up, the molecules in it spread out and it gets lighter. Warm air rises, and cooler air falls. As the air moved, your spiral and balloon had to move too.

2 Waterworks

What do you think is the most common thing in the world? Would you be surprised if we said water? That's right. Water covers about 74 percent of the Earth's surface. Not only that, you're full of it yourself! Your body is about 70 percent water, mostly locked in your cells.

All animals and plants need a steady supply of water to live. You've probably seen grass turn brown in a hot summer when there isn't much rain. And only a few specially adapted animals can live in the arid deserts. We humans use enormous amounts of water. We use it not only for drinking but also for washing, cooking, and watering crops, as well as for hydroelectric power and all sorts of factory processes.

Fortunately, the Earth's water cycle keeps water in constant circulation. Water evaporates into the air from oceans and lakes, plants and animals. Then it returns to Earth as rain or snow.

With all that water around, you'd think there'd be plenty for everybody. But there isn't. First, much of that water is not available for us to use: Most of the water on Earth is salty—and we need fresh water to drink. Water is also locked in places we can't easily get at, such as the polar ice caps and sources deep underground.

Second, water is unevenly distributed over the Earth. North Americans are fortunate to have a good supply of fresh water and the money to pipe it around. Most of us can get all the water we want just by turning on a tap. In many poorer, drier parts of the world, people have to haul water several kilometers in buckets or buy it in cans.

Third, and most important, human activities are polluting the water in lakes, rivers, and oceans. The same things that pollute the air pollute the water and water life, too. Pollution falls on water from the air or is carried down by the rain, affecting the health of everything that depends on that water—people, animals, and plants.

We don't own the water; we are part of it, and it is part of us. Our job is to take care of it, as it takes care of us. In the following activities you'll learn how to be a better caretaker of water, and you'll find out more about the wet stuff you're made of. So dive right in!

How Tall Is Your Rain?

Do you know how much it rains where you live? This simple rain gauge will give you the answer.

What you need

- A large clear plastic pop bottle
- Scissors
- An old tape measure or masking tape and a ruler
- Glue
- A thermometer
- A notebook and pen or pencil

What to do

1. Cut off the top third of the bottle.

2. Put the top in the bottle upside down to make a funnel (to keep out leaves and other large objects).

SAFETY TIP ASK AN ADULT TO HELP YOU DO THIS.

3. Measure the height of the bottle with the ruler and cut off the measuring tape at that mark. Glue it to the side. If you can't get an old tape, you can mark up a piece of masking tape in centimeters (half-inches).

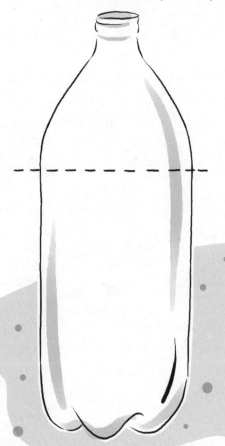

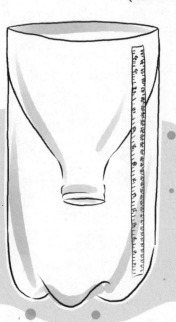

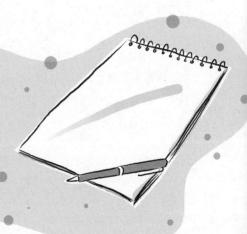

4. Find an open spot outside away from buildings and trees but where the gauge won't be knocked over. Make a hollow for it in the ground, set the gauge in the hollow, and pack some stones around it for support.

5. Check your rain gauge each time it rains. How much rain has fallen into the bottle? Record the amount in your notebook.

6. At the same time, check the temperature of the water with your thermometer. Add that information to your notes.

7. Empty the bottle after you have recorded the amount of rainfall and the temperature of the water. If it's raining a lot, you can take a reading once a day or once a week. Be sure to record the dates of your readings.

⭘More ideas . . .

• Compare your rainfall readings with those given in your newspaper or on your TV weather channel.

• Keep rain records for a month or a whole season. Make a graph of your results.

Acid Rain, Go Away!

Acid rain is rain that has dangerous chemicals such as nitrogen oxide and sulfur dioxide dissolved in it. The gases come from factory smokestacks and car exhaust. This experiment shows what can happen to plants when too much acid rain falls on them.

What you need

- 4 jars or plastic containers, all the same size (big enough to hold at least 500 mL, or 2 cups, of water), with lids
- Masking tape
- A pen or marker
- A measuring cup
- 300 mL (1¼ cups) vinegar
- 4 small, healthy potted plants, the same kind and same size
- A notebook and pen or pencil

What to do

1. Collect one jar full of rainwater.

2. Make labels for your jars from strips of masking tape. Label the jars (1) "A little acid," (2) "A lot of acid," (3) "Tap water," and (4) "Rainwater." Label your plant pots the same way.

3. Measure 50 mL (¹/₄ cup) of vinegar into jar 1 and fill the rest of the jar with tap water. Put 250 mL (1 cup) of vinegar into jar 2 and fill the rest of the jar with tap water. Fill jar 3 with straight tap water. Your jar of rainwater will be jar 4.

4. Put your plants together in a sunny place where they will get the same amount of light. Water them with the matching jars of water. Water them every few days to keep them just moist.

5. Check the plants every day for 2 or 3 weeks. Write in your notebook what you see. Do all the plants look healthy? Did the leaves droop sooner on some than on others?

What color are the leaves on different plants? When did changes start happening? Which plant started to die soonest? How does plant 4, watered with rainwater, compare with the other plants? What might that tell you about the rainfall in your area?

What's going on?

The plant that got the most acidic "rain" (plant 2) will probably wilt and die. The next sickest should be plant 1, which got a little acid. Acid rain affects plants—and animals such as fish, too—in much the same way. The more acidic the rain, the more damage it does.

☀️More ideas . . .

To see the effect of acid rain on buildings, try soaking 2 pieces of chalk overnight, 1 in vinegar and the other in water. Chalk is something like limestone, a rock used in some buildings and monuments.

A Solar Pure-Water Still

This mini version of the Earth's great water cycle makes clean (purified) water from muddy water. Called a still, it uses the same natural methods as the water cycle, too—evaporation and condensation—and it does it in a dishpan.

- Water
- A large dishpan
- Garden soil
- A drinking glass shorter than the height of the pan
- Some clean marbles
- Plastic wrap wider than the pan
- Masking tape

1. To make muddy water, put about 5 cm (2 inches) of water in the dishpan. Add a little garden soil and stir it around.

2. To make the still, set the glass right side up in the middle of the dishpan. If the glass moves around, put a few marbles in it to weigh it down.

3. Moisten the rim of the dishpan so that you can make a tight seal. Fit a piece of plastic wrap over the dishpan. Pull it smooth, but leave a tiny bit of slack. (You might want some help with this step.) Attach the plastic securely with masking tape.

4. Place a marble in the center of the plastic, directly over the glass. You want the plastic to dip down but not touch the glass.

5. Put your still outside in direct sunlight. Leave it for several hours and watch what happens.

What's going on?

The heat of the sun begins to turn the water into water vapor, a gas. The vapor rises, leaving the dirt behind. When the vapor hits the plastic, it cools because the air outside is cooler than the air inside. (The plastic has trapped heat inside the pan just like a glass roof on a greenhouse.) The water vapor condenses back into a liquid, which falls into the glass like rain. You now have "distilled" water.

Toilets 'n' Taps

Did you check out this page to see what gross experiment we had cooked up for you? Well, the following activities are gross in a way, but maybe not the way you think. They're all about the water we waste—in toilets, showers, sinks, and other places around our homes. Ready to test the waters at your home?

What you need

- A heavy, narrow, waterproof object (for example, a plastic jug)
- A large cooking pot
- A measuring cup
- A bucket
- A notebook and pen or pencil
- A watch with a second hand

What to do

PUT A JUG IN IT!

1. Ask an adult to lift the cover off the toilet tank. Flush the toilet and watch how it works. Each flush uses about 20 L (5 gallons) of water. That's more than you usually need for a flush.

2. Put a heavy object in the tank (without disturbing the mechanism). It will save a lot of wasted water. The object takes up space, so less water is needed to fill the tank.

BRUSH OFF!

1. Do you brush your teeth with the water running? Try this. Put the pot in the sink and turn on the cold water. Pretend to brush your teeth as the water runs into the pot. When you finish, turn off the tap.

2. Measure the water in the pot with your measuring cup. (Pour each cupful into the bucket. Use the water to flush the toilet or water plants.)

3. Write down how much water you used. Could you do the job with less?

LEAKIN' LIZARDS!

1. Check every tap in your home for leaks. If you find one, tighten the handle to see if it stops. If not, put it on a list to get fixed.

2. Try this test: Put your measuring cup under a tap and turn it on so that it drips. Time how long it takes to fill the cup. Multiply that by 4 to get how long it takes to drip a liter (quart). A bath can use 100 L (26 gallons) of water. How long would it take that leak to fill a bathtub?

What's going on?

It's easy to waste water, but it's easy *not* to waste it, too. You can do a perfectly good job of brushing your teeth by turning the tap on and off or filling a glass. You can have a fine shower under a water-saving showerhead that cuts water use by half. You can have a healthy lawn by giving it a good soak only once or twice a week. And if you get leaky taps fixed, you won't notice any difference at all—except that maddening *drip-drip* will be gone!

Up, Up, and Away!

Water is the Earth's great shape-shifter. It can be a liquid, a solid (ice), or a gas (water vapor). What things help it evaporate (change from a liquid to a gas)? All it takes is . . . Well, you find out.

What you need

- Measuring spoons
- 2 saucers
- 2 dish towels
- A hair dryer
- A plate
- A small bottle

What to do

1. Put 25 mL (2 tablespoons) of water into each saucer. Put 1 saucer outside in the sun. Put the other saucer in the shade. Which saucer of water evaporates faster? Why?

2. Pour 25 mL (2 tablespoons) of water into the middle of each dish towel. Spread one towel out on a table. Hold the other one up in the air. Turn the hair dryer dial to "cool" and blow air on the second towel. Which towel dries first? Why?

3. Now measure 25 mL (2 tablespoons) of water onto the plate. Put the same amount into the small bottle. Place them somewhere side by side for a few hours. This time, which container of water evaporates first? Why?

What's going on?

Water evaporates faster when it is heated, when wind blows across it, and when it is not very deep. When water is heated, the molecules pull apart and jump around. They fly off into the surrounding air as a gas, taking heat with them. Wind speeds up the process. Spreading water out helps, too. The molecules are closer to the surface and can fly off more easily.

Filtering Out the Grunge

Water in nature is never completely clean. It can contain bits of sand, dust, and minerals, as well as tiny organisms and various human-made pollutants. Filtering is just one step in making water safe to drink. Test some water samples to see what filters out.

What you need

- Several clean jars or bottles for collecting samples
- Rubber gloves
- Paper, a pen, and masking tape for making labels
- A funnel
- A large clear jar
- Coffee filters
- A notebook and pen or pencil
- A magnifying glass

What to do

1. In jars or bottles, collect several samples of water from a variety of sources, such as a pond, a lake, a well, rain, snow (let it melt), and a mud puddle. Wear rubber gloves when collecting your samples. Keep the lids on the jars so that the samples won't collect any more dirt.

SAFETY TIP
DON'T DRINK OR TOUCH ANY OF THE WATER, AND WASH YOUR HANDS CAREFULLY AFTER YOUR EXPERIMENTS. UNPURIFIED WATER CAN CONTAIN TOXIC BACTERIA.

2. Label each jar with a number and the source of the sample. Put matching numbers on the same number of filters.

4. Examine the filters with your magnifying glass. Do you see any particles? Which water was the dirtiest?

5. How well did the filtering seem to work? Do the filtered waters look clean enough to drink?

3. Place the funnel in the big jar and put in filter 1. Test your first water sample by pouring it through the filter. Set the filter aside. Wash the jar and funnel and put in filter 2. Pour your second water sample through this filter. Repeat with the other samples. Each time, compare the color, general appearance, and smell of the water before and after filtering. Write down your findings in your notebook.

 **SAFETY TIP** EVEN IF THE FILTERED WATERS LOOK CLEAN, DON'T DRINK THEM. FILTERING ONLY REMOVES LARGE PARTICLES. THE MICROSCOPIC POLLUTANTS THAT PASS THROUGH FILTERS CAN BE EVEN MORE DANGEROUS.

What's going on?

Making water safe to drink is a long process. Most towns and cities get their water from rivers, lakes, or wells. Before the water is piped into homes, water purification plants filter it and add chemicals to kill harmful bacteria. But some lakes and rivers get so polluted that the water can't be completely cleaned. Then the health of all the people, animals, and plants in the area may be affected.

More ideas . . .

Some water purification plants offer public tours. Find out if your class or you and some friends can go on one.

Crying over Spilled Oil

Accidental oil spills from ocean tankers are disasters you hear about on the news. But most oil pollution of water comes from ordinary cleaning of ships in the sea and leaking from factories on land. Either way, cleaning up oil spills is a hard job. Create a mini oil spill and see if you can do it.

What you need

- 2 tinfoil pie plates
- Food coloring
- Measuring spoons
- Cooking oil
- A feather
- Cotton rags
- A nylon stocking
- A paper towel
- Dishwashing liquid

What to do

1. Fill a pie plate halfway with water. Add a few drops of food coloring so that you'll be able to see the oil better. (Blue or green contrasts well with yellow oil.)

2. Add 2 mL (1/2 teaspoon) of oil. Does it mix with the water?

6. Now half-fill the other plate with water and create an oil spill. Add about 2 mL (¹/₂ teaspoon) of dishwashing liquid. What happens this time? Where does the oil go? Is the water clean now?

3. Create a wind by blowing gently across the water. What do you think happens to oily water in a storm?

4. Drag the feather through the oil. How do you think birds are affected by oil spills?

5. Try to clean up the oil spill in the water with a cotton rag. Next, try the nylon stocking and then a paper towel. (Add more oil if needed.) Which one works best? Can you get all the oil cleaned up?

What's going on?

Real oil spills are very damaging to water plants and animals. The thick oil coats birds' feathers so that they can't fly. Shellfish caught in an oil spill can't reproduce. And cleanup methods are not perfect. Chemicals that act like detergents break up the oil into smaller droplets, but the toxins from the oil are still in the environment. And often the chemical detergents are pollutants, too. Soaking up the oil with absorbent materials such as cotton and nylon is expensive and slow. What happens to the oil that doesn't get cleaned up?

Make Your Own "Green" Cleaners

Store-bought cleaners may contain chemicals that are harmful to health or that pollute the environment. But you can mix up some safe, natural products that work just as well and are cheaper, too. Create a personal line of products and use them to clean your own home.

What you need

- Empty spray bottles
- A small jar
- A measuring cup
- Measuring spoons
- Paper
- Pens, markers, or colored pencils
- White craft glue or tape

What to do

GLASS CLEANER

Pour vinegar into a spray bottle until it's half full. Fill the bottle with water and shake to mix. Use the paper and pens, markers, or colored pencils to make a label that says: "Apply with newspaper." Attach the label to the bottle with glue or tape.

FURNITURE POLISH

- 15 mL (1 tablespoon) olive oil
- 10 mL (2 teaspoons) vinegar or lemon juice
- 500 mL (2 cups) warm water

Mix ingredients in a spray bottle. Instructions for label: "For varnished wood. Heat mixture by setting bottle in pan of hot water. Shake bottle after heating. Apply polish to wood and rub dry with a soft cloth."

SILVER POLISH

- 25 mL (2 tablespoons) baking soda
- 25 mL (2 tablespoons) salt
- A piece of aluminum foil

Mix ingredients in a small jar. Instructions for label: "Add 10 ml (2 teaspoons) to 1 L (1 quart) of warm water. Add a small piece of foil. Soak silverware or silver jewelry in this solution. Replace foil when it turns black."

💡 More ideas . . .

- **Make colorful labels for your products. Besides the instructions, the labels could have clever names for your cleaners. You could also list the ingredients. Add that they are kind to the earth. Glue or tape the labels on the containers. For a gift, you could put all your cleaners in a basket.**

- **Conduct a test. Clean half of an item with your product and the other half with a store-bought cleaner. Compare how long it took to clean the item, how hard it was, and what the results were.**

3 Earthborn

Just as you have air and water inside you all the time, you have earth (also known as soil or dirt) inside you, too. You probably don't eat dirt directly (at least you probably haven't since you were a little kid). But you do eat it indirectly every day, because almost all your food comes from the soil.

We're not going to explain exactly how that happens, because you'll find out for yourself if you do the first activity. But the soil really does give us all our food, so it's pretty important stuff.

Did you know that soil starts out as rock? It takes millions of years for it to wear down to sand and clay. And that still isn't the kind of soil we need for growing food crops. When you do these activities, you'll discover what else soil needs to become fertile topsoil. Nature creates topsoil all the time, but at a very slow pace—it takes 500 years for just 2.5 cm (1 inch) to form! Only 8 percent of the Earth's surface is covered with that kind of soil. So you can see how precious it is.

Everything in the world is related, remember? So sometimes the poisons that go into air and water seep down into the ground as well. Soil can also become polluted by the mountains of garbage we produce. Dangerous waste is thrown on the ground or buried underground with city trash and just stays there for decades or longer. Chemicals can leak into the ground and from there seep into water wells and fields where food is grown.

Another danger to soil is erosion. Soil wears away naturally when wind and rain sweep across it. In time, new topsoil forms. But today topsoil is being lost faster than it can form again. Huge factory-like farms plant too many crops and grow the same kinds over and over without giving the soil time to rest. That uses up the nutrients in the soil, and when they're all gone, nothing can grow in it.

Valuable farmland can also be gobbled up when cities grow bigger or big dams are built. Then whole ecosystems can be lost. The Earth is made up of a great variety of ecosystems, including boreal forests, wetlands, prairie grasslands, tundra, tropical rain forests, deserts, and oceans. In an ecosystem, plants, animals, water, and soil work together in a close relationship. If even one part of an ecosystem is lost or damaged, all the other parts are threatened.

As you try some of the experiments and projects in this chapter, you'll learn more about soil and how it can be harmed. But you'll also learn how to take care of it and use it well. Happy digging!

Kitchen Sleuth

Plop on your detective cap and get ready to solve the Mystery of Where Food Comes From. Okay, it comes from a grocery store—but where does the store get it? You might have seen lettuce or tomatoes growing in a garden. But what about ice cream, bran flakes, and salami?

What you need

- A notebook with unlined pages
- A pencil or pen
- Some reference books

What to do

1. Take a tour of your kitchen food supplies. Check the refrigerator, freezer, and food cupboards. Pick 3 to 5 foods you'd like to find out about and write their names in your notebook. Allow 2 or 3 pages for each food.

2. If possible, write down the name of the country each food came from. Look for it on a sticker or on the food's package if it has one. (It might say "Made in ..." or "A product of ...")

3. If you've chosen a food in a box, can, jar, or other package, read the small print to find out if it is a mixture of different foods. List all of these ingredients in your notebook.

4. Look for information about each food, using dictionaries, encyclopedias, library books, or the Internet. Write down how the food grows (for example, on a tree) or was produced, plus 2 or 3 other interesting facts about it.

5. If a food contains several ingredients, follow each back to its beginnings. For example, if a can of pudding has cornstarch in it, find out where cornstarch comes from. Some of those ingredients with strange names may be chemicals. Sometimes you can find out why they were added to the food (for example, to keep it fresh longer). If you can't find out anything more about them, just write down "chemical."

6. Decorate each food "chapter" with drawings or magazine pictures of the food or its ingredients. What surprises did you discover? Did you find many foods that contained lots of chemicals? What do you notice about the origin of all the foods you've studied?

What's going on?

If you solve the case, you'll find that every food (except some of those chemicals) came from plants, which were grown in the soil. Even meat begins in the earth, because food animals eat seeds and grains.

More ideas . . .

- **Research the foods in your favorite meal.**

- **Next time you're in a supermarket, notice the different food departments—fruits and vegetables, meat, fish, deli, frozen foods, dairy, bakery, packaged foods. Choose a food from each of 3 or 4 departments to research.**

- **Ask your teacher or parents if they could arrange for you and your friends to take a tour of a farm or a food-processing factory.**

Get the Dirt on Dirt

You know that stuff you walk on every day? No, not the floor, sidewalk, or pavement. If you're lucky, you get to walk on the earth—that is, the ground or soil. You know it well, but do you know what's in it? The next two activities will give you a good idea.

What you need

- Some garden soil
- A cooking pot (clear, if possible) and lid
- Masking tape
- A medium-sized clear glass jar
- A marker or pen
- A tall glass jar with a screw-top lid

What to do

1. Put a 2.5-cm (1-inch) layer of soil in the pot. Put on the lid and heat the pot slowly on a stove at low heat. Look inside and write down what happens.

   SAFETY TIP ASK AN ADULT TO HELP YOU USE THE STOVE.

2. Fasten a piece of tape vertically along the outside of the medium-sized jar. Fill the jar halfway with soil and mark the level on the tape. Fill the jar with water. Don't stir it; just let it stand uncovered. Watch what happens. In about half an hour, mark the soil level on the tape again. Has it changed? Write down the reason you think this happened.

3. Now fill about one-quarter of the tall jar with soil. Add water almost to the top. Screw the lid on firmly. Shake the jar really hard for about 1 minute. Place it where you can watch it for a few days. Again, write down what happens.

4. Look at your notes. Can you list at least 4 things that you've discovered are in the soil?

What's going on?

Here are some clues: In step 1, you should see little drops on the inner sides of the pot. In step 2, bubbles will form on the surface of the water and the soil level will change. In step 3, the soil will gradually settle into 4 separate layers, from heaviest to lightest. Still not sure what's happening? See the answer at the bottom of the page.

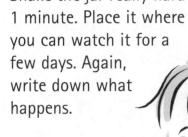

ANSWER
The drops are water. The bubbles are air (the soil level went down because air between the particles escaped into the water). And the layers should be gravel on the bottom, then sand, then clay and silt, and finally humus (dead plants and soil animals) on top.

Make Your Own Soil

It takes many years for nature to make soil. But you can do the job in just a few minutes.

What you need

- Several small rocks
- A thick cloth bag or piece of cloth
- Safety goggles
- A hammer
- A small plastic bag
- Bits of old, dead plants
- Moss
- Some small dead insects
- Pieces of rotting wood
- A small pot or container
- Some seeds (for example, grass, beans, radishes, marigolds)

What to do

1. Put the rocks in the bag or wrap them in the cloth. Turn all the open edges under. Put the bag on the ground or on a big rock.

   SAFETY TIP ASK AN ADULT TO HELP YOU WITH THE NEXT PART.

2. Put on your goggles, because you are going to smash those rocks to smithereens! Keep hammering the rocks until you have ground them into the smallest possible bits.

3. Collect some dead leaves, moss, dead insects, and bits of crumbly, rotting wood in the plastic bag. Shred the plants if they are in large pieces.

4. Pour the crushed rock into the plastic bag. (Ask someone to hold it open for you.) Add a spoonful or two of water. Now mash and squish the bag until the ingredients are well mixed. How does it look? If needed, add more water or more dead plants. You might want to add some compost (see page 66). You now have soil!

5. Try out your soil. Pack it into a small pot or a container and plant some seeds. Put the container in a sunny spot and keep the soil moist. So how does your garden grow?

What's going on?

Wind, rain, blowing sand, and plants wear down rock over many years. The fine bits mix with decayed plants and animals that fall to Earth and make the fertile soil we need for life.

☉ More ideas . . .

Try growing some seeds in crushed rock alone. Compare your 2 growing soils. Which one worked best?

Journey under the Earth

Put on your spacesuits! Okay, just kidding. But you will be going underground—half a meter (20 inches) below the surface of the soil. That might not seem like much, but you'll discover that things are very different down under.

What you need

- A small shovel or trowel
- Topsoil from a garden
- 2 large plastic containers
- Subsoil from about 50 cm (20 inches) down in the ground
- Newspapers
- A magnifying glass
- 2 small empty cans
- 2 bean seeds

What to do

1. Collect a scoopful of garden soil and put it into one of the plastic containers. Get permission before digging.

2. A good place to get subsoil is from a bank or ditch where the soil has been cut or worn away. Or you can dig a hole in your garden. Again, get permission first. Put a scoopful of subsoil into the second container.

3. Spread newspapers on a flat surface and carefully examine your 2 samples. Use a magnifying glass if you have one. How are the soils different? Which do you think would be better for growing plants in?

4. Now fill 1 can with topsoil and the other with subsoil. Soak the bean seeds in water overnight and then plant 1 in each can. Water both cans lightly and put them in a sunny spot. Keep the soils moist. Watch the plants for several days. Which plant is stronger? Was your prediction right?

What's going on?

Subsoil contains more stones and less humus, or organic matter (dead leaves, roots, twigs, and soil animals), than topsoil. So it isn't very good for growing plants. Topsoil contains what plants need to thrive—organic matter and microscopic organisms such as bacteria to break it down.

Worm World

Who says earthworms are icky? They're really amazing gardeners, because they help make soil rich and fertile for growing plants. But don't take our word for it. Make this wormery and watch it happen.

What you need

- 2 sheets of clear acrylic plastic, about 30 cm (12 inches) square (get these at a hardware or home building store)
- 3 pieces of wood, about 30 cm x 7.5 cm x 1 cm (12 inches x 3 inches x $\frac{1}{2}$ inch)
- A piece of heavy cardboard about 30 cm x 10 cm (12 inches x 4 inches) for a cover
- Strong tape
- Several kinds of soil (for example, garden soil, fine gravel, sand)
- 8 to 10 earthworms
- Dry leaves or grass clippings
- Dark cloth or an opened-up garbage bag

What to do

1. Tape the plastic and wood together as shown in the picture.

SAFETY TIP
YOU'LL PROBABLY NEED AN ADULT TO HELP WITH THIS.

2. Fill the wormery with layers of different kinds of soil. Make every second layer garden soil and end with garden soil. Sprinkle a bit of water over each layer as you add it. You want the soil to be damp but not wet.

3. Get some worms (see below).

4. Place the worms on the top layer of the wormery. They'll probably start burrowing underground right away.

5. Spread some leaves or grass on top for the worms to eat. Use leaves near where you found the worms.

6. Put the lid on so that the wormery won't dry out. Except when you're studying it, keep it covered with a dark cloth—worms are night creatures. Water your wormery every so often to keep it moist. Watch what happens over several days.

7. When you've finished studying your worms, free them where you found them.

What's going on?

As earthworms burrow around in the soil, they loosen it up and mix in air. They also fertilize it by pulling in dead plants and excreting worm casts (dung).

Two ways to collect worms

At night: Take a flashlight and hand rake to a lawn after dark. If you don't see any worms on the grass, carefully dig in the soil.

During the day: Stir a spoonful of dishwashing liquid into a large watering can full of water. Pour the mixture over a patch of grass about a meter (a yard) square. In a few minutes, some worms should come to the surface. Gently rinse them in fresh water before putting them in your wormery.

More ideas . . .

- Keep a daily log of what happens in your wormery. Study it with a magnifying glass.

- Make a careful drawing of a worm.

What a Load of Rubbish!

When the garbage truck hauls away your trash, that's not the end of it. Most of it gets buried underground in giant landfills. Then what happens to it? Build a mini landfill and find out.

What you need

- A large cardboard box
- Large garbage bags
- Tape
- Garden soil
- 6 to 8 samples to test (small, similar-sized pieces)—for example, potato peelings, crushed eggshells, plastic bag, pop can, Styrofoam cup, tinfoil, 100 percent cotton cloth, nylon stocking, newspaper, shiny magazine cover, small glass bottle
- Gardening or rubber gloves
- Popsicle sticks
- A notebook and pen or pencil

What to do

1. Line the box with garbage bags. Tape them together. Fill the box halfway with soil.

2. Bury each sample about 15 cm (6 inches) deep in the soil. Wear your gloves when handling soil (it has bacteria in it). Mark each spot with a popsicle stick.

3. Put the box in a warm, sunny place and water it lightly. Keep the soil moist but not soaked.

4. Dig up your samples every week or so and check them carefully. You can use a magnifying glass if you have one. Keep checking for 2 or 3 months. In your notebook, write down what you see.

5. Which items break down quickly? Which take a long time to rot? Are there some things that look as if they'll never rot?

What's going on?

Bacteria, fungi, and worms in soil will break down or "biodegrade" organic material (dead plants and animals and things made from them) and form new soil. (That is, they will if there's enough air and moisture. Newspapers you could still read have been dug up after being buried 30 years in a landfill!) Materials that are not found in nature, such as plastic and glass, will never biodegrade. A pop can tossed on the ground will take 300 years to be crushed and worn away by rocks; a glass bottle will take a million years.

More ideas . . .

- Plant your samples outside. Ask for permission before you dig.

- Collect neighborhood litter as samples. Wearing your gloves, pick up a few items and put each in a plastic bag. Punch lots of holes in the bags and bury them in your landfill. Predict which things will rot fastest and slowest.

Tempest in a Cake Pan

All life depends on soil. But rain or too much irrigation can wash away precious topsoil that has taken years to form. Some conditions make that erosion more likely to happen. Try these experiments to see soil erosion—and soil protection—in action.

What you need

- 3 disposable tinfoil cake pans, 2 L size (9 inches x 12 inches)
- Plastic wrap
- Tape
- Garden soil
- Grass seed
- Newspapers
- A large cookie sheet
- 2 small jars with metal screw lids
- 2 wood blocks

What to do

1. Punch small holes all over one end of each pan, as in the picture below.

   SAFETY TIP ASK AN ADULT TO USE A HAMMER AND NAIL TO PUNCH THE HOLES IN THE PANS.

2. Cover the holes in one pan with plastic wrap taped to the outside. At the same time, punch a few holes in the jar lids to make watering cans.

   SAFETY TIP ASK AN ADULT TO PUNCH THESE HOLES, TOO.

3. Fill the covered-end pan with loose garden soil almost to the top. Scatter grass seed on top and press it into the soil. Water the pan and place it in a sunny spot. Put newspapers underneath to catch any drips. Water your "crop" once or twice a day to keep the soil moist.

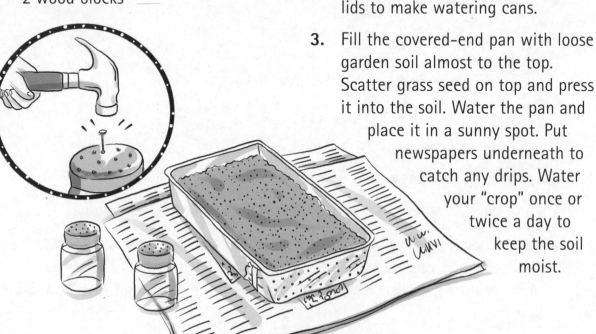

4. When you have a nice patch of grass (in 2 to 3 weeks), remove the plastic end cover. Fill a second pan with loose soil. Place the pierced ends of both pans on the cookie sheet. Put a block of wood or other prop under the opposite end of each pan so that the pans are slanted at the same angle.

5. Fill the jars with water. Gently water the 2 pans at the same time. What happens to the soil? How much water and soil from each pan run off onto the cookie sheet?

6. Now fill the third pan with loose soil. Replace the soil in the second pan with fresh soil. (Save the wet soil to use for plants.) Set up these two pans on the cookie sheet the same as before.

7. This time use a spoon handle or your finger to trace a series of straight furrows down one pan. In the other pan, trace one long S-shaped furrow curving back and forth across the pan. Farmers call this pattern contour plowing. Water your fields. What happens?

More ideas . . .

Try terrace farming. Tilt 2 freshly filled pans up on the cookie tin. In 1 pan, work the soil into a series of terraces, facing the end with the holes. Water the pans. Why is terrace farming a good idea in countries with hills and heavy rainfall?

Rambling Roots

All living things have a built-in will to survive. When their environment changes, they try hard to adapt. Plants often do amazing things to find what they need to grow. Read over this experiment before you try it and write down what you think the roots of the plants will do.

What you need

- Scissors
- 2 large clear plastic pop bottles
- A permanent-ink marker
- Coarse sand
- Garden soil
- Bean seeds
- 2 saucers

What you do

1. Cut off about the top third of each bottle.

2. Punch several small holes in the bottom of each bottle so that water can drain out.

SAFETY TIP ASK AN ADULT TO USE THE SCISSORS TO PUNCH THE HOLES IN THE BOTTLES.

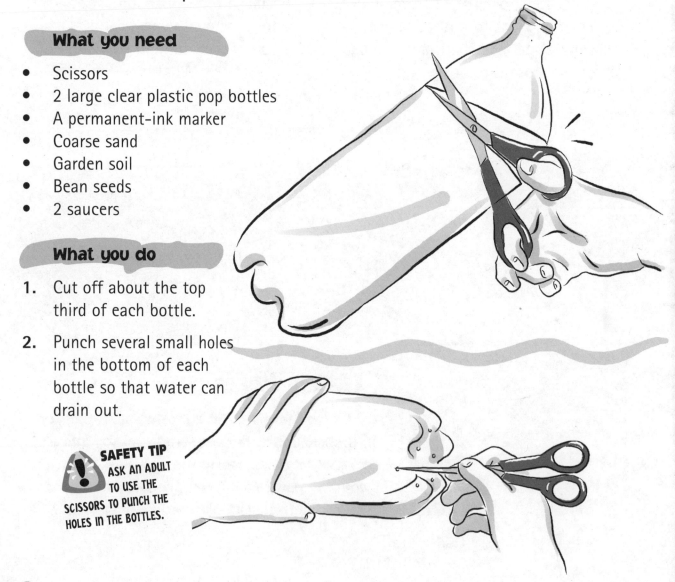

6. Plant 4 or 5 bean seeds along the sides of each bottle. Push the seeds into the garden soil about 2 cm (³/₄ inch) below the surface.

7. Put the bottles in a sunny place. Put saucers under them to catch the drips. Water them often to keep the soil moist but not soaked. In a few days the beans will germinate and start to grow.

3. Use a marker to label the bottles 1 and 2.

4. Fill each bottle about halfway with sand.

5. In bottle 1, add a layer of garden soil about 7.5 cm (3 inches) deep. In bottle 2, add a layer of garden soil 2.5 cm (1 inch deep).

8. Watch what happens to the roots of the plants in each bottle. Is there a difference between how they grow in shallow and in deeper soil? Why do you think this happens? Was your prediction right?

Composter Can

Don't toss your veggie peels—compost them. Composting not only uses up a lot of garbage but helps gardens bloom, too. If you don't already have a composter at home, here's how to make one.

What you need

- A plastic garbage can, with a top
- Garden soil
- Grass clippings and dry leaves
- Kitchen scraps such as vegetable and fruit peelings, crushed eggshells, coffee grounds, and tea bags (no meat, fish, bones, or dairy products, since they attract animals such as rodents and raccoons)
- A long stick for stirring
- Optional: soil animals (for example, red worms, sow bugs)

What you do

1. Remove the bottom of the can.

 SAFETY TIP ASK AN ADULT TO DO THIS PART.

2. Drill some holes in the side of the garbage can.

 **SAFETY TIP** ASK AN ADULT TO DRILL THE HOLES IN THE CAN.

3. Find a convenient, sunny spot outside not too close to a wall. Push the can firmly down into the soil. If the soil is too hard, cut a trench for the can with a trowel.

4. Put a thin layer of garden soil on the bottom of the can. Add some yard waste and then your kitchen scraps. To speed up the rotting process, shred or chop up the scraps. Add another layer of grass or leaves and finish with a layer of garden soil. Add the soil animals if you're using them.

5. Stir the compost. Add a sprinkle of water if it's too dry or add some soil if it's too wet. Keep it just damp. Put the top on.

6. Now you have somewhere to put your food scraps. Every time you add some, toss in more grass cuttings and soil. Stir every few days.

7. When your composter is about 3/4 full, stop adding to it and just let it work. In a few weeks you should have some rich, dark compost for your garden or houseplants. Or give it to a neighbor or friend.

What's going on?

Bacteria, fungi, worms, and other "decomposers" in the soil break down organic matter and turn it into food for new plants.

Forest in a Jar

You may live far from a real forest, but you can create a mini forest habitat right in your own room.

What you need

- 3 or 4 small plants
- A trowel
- A large clear-glass jar with a wide mouth
- Small stones
- Gardening charcoal (buy from a garden center)
- A nylon stocking
- Garden soil that contains vermiculite and peat moss
- Aquarium sand (get this from a pet supply store)
- A kitchen funnel
- Optional: tiny pieces of driftwood or log, pebbles, pine needles, or other forest litter

What to do

1. Collect your plants. Be sure to choose plants that won't grow too big for your jar, such as mosses, miniature ivy, and tiny flowering plants. Be very gentle and take only plants that are plentiful. Use your trowel to dig up each plant's entire root and the soil it's clinging to.

2. Wash, rinse, and dry your jar well.

6. Decide where you want your plants—don't crowd them. Now poke holes in the soil and add a little water to each. Remove as much soil from the roots of the plants as you can. Then carefully plant them in the holes. Press the soil down and water it lightly. Add any forest litter you've collected to decorate the scene.

7. Place the jar near a window but not in direct sunlight. Keep the lid on and add water only when the habitat looks dry.

What's going on?

Your forest should create its own water cycle—the plants draw moisture up with their roots and send it into the air through the leaves. Moisture collects on the lid and falls back down as "rain."

💡 More ideas . . .

- **You might want to make a more elaborate forest in an aquarium. For the soil, measure 10 parts soil to 1 part sand and 1 part charcoal. Seal the top securely with plastic wrap.**

- **Instead of a forest, create a field habitat using small wild grasses and tiny flowers.**

3. Wash the stones and charcoal. Put a 2.5-cm (1-inch) layer of stones in the bottom of the jar. Cover with a layer of charcoal about 1 cm (¹/₂ inch) deep. The charcoal will filter the water.

4. Cut up the stocking and cover the charcoal with several pieces. They will keep the soil from drifting into the charcoal.

5. Mix together about 150 mL (²/₃ cup) garden soil, 15 mL (1 tablespoon) charcoal, and 15 mL (1 tablespoon) aquarium sand. Pour the mixture into the jar through the funnel to keep the sides of the jar clean.

Fake Fossils

Fossils are traces of plants or animals left in the Earth's crust millions of years ago. Most fossils are petrified (turned to stone) or are imprints found in rock. Real fossils take thousands of years to form, but you can make fake versions in a few minutes. Try these methods to "fossilize" animal footprints, leaves, or flowers.

SUNKEN GARDEN

What you need

- Modeling clay
- A rolling pin
- Leaves, flowers, or other natural items to "fossilize"
- A table knife
- Optional: food coloring

What to do

1. If you want a colored print, mix food coloring into the clay first. Then roll out a chunk of clay until it's about 2 cm ($3/4$ inch) thick.

2. Center a leaf or other item, vein-side down, on the clay. Press it firmly into the clay with the rolling pin. Remove the leaf. You might want to cut off the edges of the clay to make a circle, square, or other shape. Use the same method to make as many prints as you like.

3. Bake your fossil in the oven, at the lowest temperature, until it hardens—1 or 2 hours.

SAFETY TIP
ASK AN ADULT TO HELP YOU BAKE THE FOSSIL.

RAISE YOUR PAWS

What you need

- Tape
- A piece of cardboard about 10 cm x 30 cm (4 inches x 12 inches)
- Plaster of Paris
- A small bowl or plastic container
- A jar of water
- A stirring stick or spoon

What to do

1. Go for a hike with your materials in a backpack. Look for animal footprints where there is soft, damp soil, such as near a riverbank or along a forest path after it has rained.

2. When you find a clear print, gently brush away any leaves, stones, or loose dirt. Tape the cardboard strip into a ring. Center it over the print and push it firmly into the soil.

3. Spoon a little plaster of Paris into the bowl or plastic container. Slowly stir in water until you have a soft, thick mixture something like toothpaste. Spoon out over the print to a depth of about 3 cm (a little over an inch) and smooth it. Let it harden—about half an hour.

4. Carefully lift up the mold. You will have a raised impression of the footprint for your fossil collection.

5. Be sure to take all your materials home with you.

A Very Veggie Chili

Growing vegetables, grains, and fruit uses up less land and energy than raising animals for food. And not only is vegetarian food good for you and the planet, it's also delicious.

What you need

(for 3 servings)

1	small onion, chopped
1	celery stalk, chopped
1/2	green pepper, chopped
1	small carrot, chopped
1	clove garlic, diced
4	mushrooms, thinly sliced
375 mL (1 1/2 cups)	canned tomatoes, chopped, including juice
1 540-mL (19-ounce)	can red kidney beans
250 mL (1 cup)	vegetable stock (made from a bouillon cube)
25 mL (2 tablespoons)	vegetable oil
250 mL (1 cup)	corn kernels, raw, frozen, or canned
2 mL (1/2 teaspoon)	salt
5 mL (1 teaspoon)	oregano
7 mL (1 1/2 teaspoons)	chili powder
5 mL (1 teaspoon)	cumin

- A knife
- A measuring cup
- Measuring spoons
- A colander
- 2 small mixing bowls
- A potato masher or fork
- A large pot or wok
- A wooden spoon

What to do

1. First, get all the vegetables ready. Chop the onion, celery, green pepper, and carrot into small pieces. Chop the garlic into very small pieces. Slice the mushrooms. Chop the tomatoes a bit.

SAFETY TIP
ASK AN ADULT TO HELP YOU MAKE THIS. (BETTER ASK A FRIEND, TOO—YOU'LL BE DOING A LOT OF CHOPPING!)

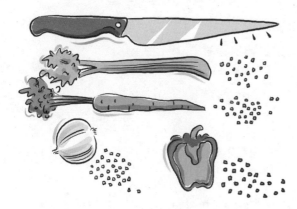

2. Pour the beans into the colander and rinse them under cold running water. Put 250 mL (1 cup) of the beans into one of the bowls and mash them with a potato masher or fork.

3. In the other bowl, crumble a vegetable bouillon cube and pour 250 mL (1 cup) of boiling water over it. Stir and let it dissolve.

4. In the pot, heat the oil over medium heat. Add the onion and garlic. Fry them gently for 2 or 3 minutes, stirring a few times.

5. Add the celery, green pepper, carrot, and mushrooms. Cook 3 to 5 minutes or until tender, stirring a few times.

6. Add the tomatoes, beans (mashed and whole), stock, corn, salt, oregano, chili powder, and cumin. Stir.

7. Cover the pot and turn the heat to low. Let the chili cook gently for 30 minutes. If it's still too watery, take off the cover and cook another 10 minutes or so.

💡 More ideas . . .

- **Put grated cheese on top before you serve your chili—unless you want a vegan meal. That's one without animal products of any kind. (Cheese is made from milk, which comes from cows.)**

- **For a complete meal, eat this chili with brown rice or corn tortillas.**

It's Superbean!

What do a bean and the Man of Steel have in common? They both get dressed in a phone booth. Just kidding! But this is no joke: Beans can break rocks. Try this.

What you need

- 4 or 5 dried beans
- A waxed milk carton
- A knife
- Garden soil
- Plaster of Paris
- A tin can or plastic container
- A small glass jar with a screw-top lid
- A plastic container with a lid

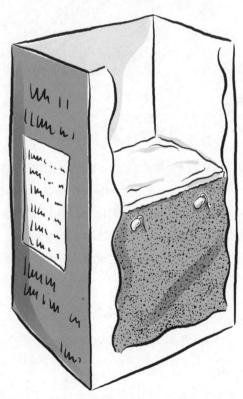

What to do

1. Soak the beans overnight in water.

2. Wash the inside of the milk carton and cut off the top.

SAFETY TIP
ASK AN ADULT TO CUT OFF THE TOP.

3. Fill the carton halfway with soil. Water the soil until it is completely damp but not soaked.

4. Plant the beans about 2 cm (3/4 inch) beneath the surface of the soil. Don't crowd them.

5. Spoon a little plaster of Paris into a can or plastic container. Add just enough water to make a paste you can pour. Cover the soil in the carton with a thin layer of plaster. It will harden in a few minutes. Set the carton aside for several days. What happens?

6. Pack the glass jar with as many beans as you can squeeze in. Fill it up with water. Screw the lid on tightly.

7. Put the jar in the plastic container and close the lid. Let it sit for a few days. What happens?

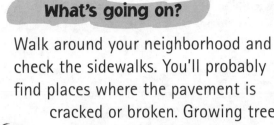

What's going on?

Walk around your neighborhood and check the sidewalks. You'll probably find places where the pavement is cracked or broken. Growing tree roots have created enough pressure to cause the cracks. When plants grow and expand, they really are strong enough to crack rock. (They can crack plaster and glass, too.) Plants are one of the forces that over a very long time wear down rock into soil.

4 All Fired Up

You know where the sun is. It's 150 million km (93 million miles) out there in space. It's certainly not inside your body like air, water, and earth.

Or so you might think. In fact, you do have the sun inside you in the form of energy. All life on Earth needs energy from the sun. Plants use the sun's energy to grow, and some of that energy is passed on to you when you eat fruits and vegetables. The same thing happens when you eat a hamburger, which is made from a cow. The cow eats grain that grew in the sun, then the sun's energy passes from the grain to the cow to you.

Food is your fuel. It gives you the energy to shoot hoops or even take a nap. The energy from coal, gas, oil, and running water—fuels that run factories and automobiles—came from the sun, too. Life would just stop if we didn't have the sun constantly recharging our batteries.

Nature has a perfect way of using energy without producing any leftover garbage, or waste. For instance, an apple tree uses energy from sunlight to grow and produce apples. The apples that aren't picked fall to the ground and rot, providing food for small animals and making the soil richer for other plants to grow. Nothing is wasted. All plants and animals—except humans—use energy in a circular pattern like that, called a food chain.

Humans are the only animals that use energy and produce waste, and we're extremely good at it! Then we have to figure out what to do with that waste. Much of it, including pollutants, ends up in the air, in the water, or buried underground.

Part of the problem is that we're using too much coal, gas, and oil—fuels that not only pollute but will run out. They were formed over billions of years from the remains of ancient plants and animals, and there is only a certain amount of them. After they are used, they are gone forever. We can't use them over and over, like water, and we can't plant new ones, as we can with trees. Sources of energy such as water and wood, which can be replaced, are called renewable resources. Sources such as coal, gas, and oil, which can't be replaced, are known as nonrenewable resources.

Another problem with coal, gas, and oil is that when you burn them, they release carbon dioxide. This is not a dangerous gas in normal amounts. But we've poured so much of it into the air that it's forming a blanket around the Earth, trapping heat. And that trapped heat may be warming up the Earth's air. Warmer temperatures might not sound like a bad thing, but the effects can be very serious.

Much is being done to try to solve our energy problems. Some governments are passing laws to cut down the amount of carbon dioxide that factories are allowed to release. Scientists are developing cleaner fuels and testing renewable energy sources such as wind, tides, and the sun's direct power itself. And everyone can do simple things to save energy.

In this chapter and the next chapter, you'll explore some energy questions and watch the sun in action. Ready to play in the sun?

Jungle Gymnastics

In this experiment, you'll be giving a plant a workout. You're going to hang it upside down! Find out what a plant does when the world is suddenly topsy-turvy.

What you need

- A table knife
- A small potted plant with sturdy roots
- 2 large sponges
- Strong cord

What to do

1. Run the knife around the inside of the pot to loosen the ball of soil. Carefully remove the plant from the pot, keeping as much soil clinging to the roots as you can.

2. Moisten the sponges and wrap one of them on each side of the root ball, tying them on securely with cord. If the plant is heavy, you might also have to tie a cord vertically (up and down) around the root ball.

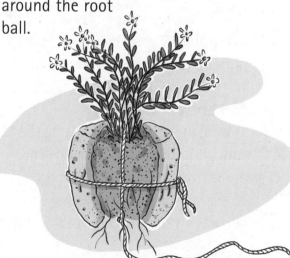

3. Tie a long piece of cord to the sponge cord. Hang the plant upside down from a plant hook or a hook on a ledge near a sunny window. You might want to spread newspaper to protect the carpet or floor.

4. Keep the sponges moist and watch the plant for a week or two. Predict what you think will happen. What *does* happen? Why do you think the plant reacted the way it did?

What's going on?

Plant stems are heliotropic—they grow toward the sun. Roots are geotropic—they reach for the Earth. So if necessary, plants will twist themselves into all kinds of strange shapes to get what they need. As their roots draw nourishment from the soil and their leaves pull energy from the sun, plants are bridges between Earth and the heavens.

Make a Solar Water Heater

The sun is a source of endlessly renewable, pollution-free energy. The trick is to find practical ways to use it. Solar panels are a great way to provide heating and hot water for buildings. Of course, you need to live in a sunny place! You need a sunny day for this experiment, too.

What you need

- Scissors
- A black plastic garbage bag
- 3 tinfoil cake pans, all the same size
- Masking tape
- A measuring cup
- Plastic wrap
- A thermometer
- A saucer
- A notebook and pen or pencil

What to do

SAFETY TIP REMEMBER, NEVER LOOK DIRECTLY AT THE SUN.

1. Start around 10:00 A.M., when the sun is moving overhead. Cut off a piece of garbage bag big enough to line one of the cake pans. Line the pan and tape the bag securely in place.

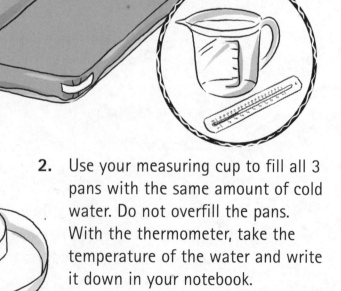

2. Use your measuring cup to fill all 3 pans with the same amount of cold water. Do not overfill the pans. With the thermometer, take the temperature of the water and write it down in your notebook.

3. Fasten plastic wrap securely over the top of the pan lined with black plastic and one of the other pans. Leave the third pan uncovered.

4. Place the 3 pans outside in a sunny spot. Let them sit in the sun for 3 or 4 hours.

5. Check the pans every hour. Each time, take the temperature of the water in each pan, beginning with the uncovered pan. Write these measurements in your notebook beside the times you checked.

6. Compare your readings. Does the water heat faster in one pan than in the others? Which pan of water got the hottest? Why do you think it did? Which pan was the solar panel? Was it helpful to have the other pans in the experiment? Why?

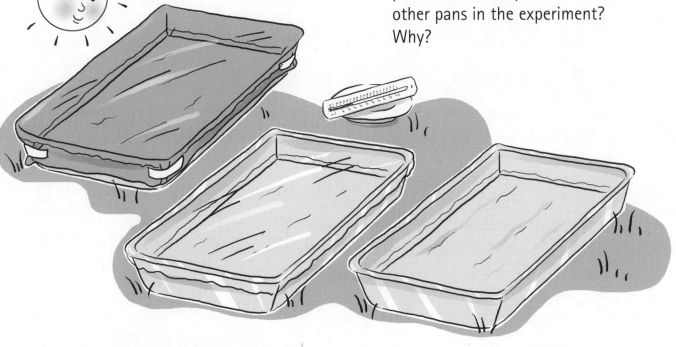

What's going on?

Solar panels in roofs are boxes with a black plate on the bottom and glass or plastic over the top. Black absorbs more heat than other colors. (Isn't a white T-shirt cooler on a hot day than a black one?) The plastic or glass top traps heat inside the box, just as it does on a greenhouse. Air or water can flow through the box in pipes and be carried throughout the house.

Magic Candle

Do you know why a candle keeps burning? When you light a candle, the match flame passes heat energy to the candle's wick. The hot wax then combines with oxygen in the air and produces carbon dioxide and water vapor. That's called a chemical reaction. The reaction produces more heat, which keeps the candle burning. You can use this reaction to create a sizzling ending for a magic show (see page 25).

What you need

- A tall, straight-sided candle (not dripless)
- A small knife
- A ruler
- 2 metal skewers or nails
- 2 large equal-sized tin cans or plastic tubs and their tops
- Matches

What to do

1. Trim some wax off the bottom of the candle so that the wick sticks out.

2. Measure the length of the candle and find the center. At the center point, push the skewers in, one on each side. Don't push them through to the wick or the candle might break.

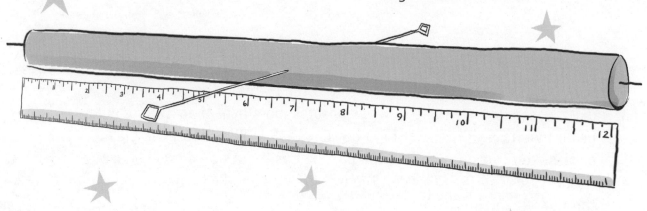

3. Balance the skewers on the edges of the cans, as shown in the picture. The candle should be straight. If one end dips, trim it until the candle balances. Place the can tops under the ends of the candle to catch the drips. You are now ready for your performance.

4. Tell your audience that you will use fire power to make a perpetual-motion machine. Light both ends of the candle. Your magic candle will soon begin to seesaw up and down. It will keep on going until the whole candle is burned. Sha-zaam!

What's going on?

One end of the candle will soon drip more wax than the other. That makes it lighter, so it goes up. The end that goes down drips a big blob, so it becomes lighter and goes back up. And on and on...

💡 More ideas . . .

For more flash, decorate your tin cans. Paint designs on them or make paper labels. Trace around the original labels to get the right size. You might want to draw fiery designs on them such as lightning bolts, suns, and stars.

Gases in Glasses

Scientists believe that the Earth is getting warmer. One reason is that too much carbon dioxide, from factories and car exhaust, is building up in the atmosphere. This experiment shows how that heats things up.

What you need

- 2 large glass jars that are the same size
- 2 pieces of dark paper or cloth
- 2 thermometers
- 1 jar lid
- A notebook and pen or pencil
- Oven mitts

What to do

SAFETY TIP
DO NOT LOOK DIRECTLY AT THE SUN.

1. Lay the jars on their sides outdoors in the sun. Put a piece of paper or cloth inside each jar.

2. Place a thermometer in each jar on top of the dark paper or cloth. This will help you read the thermometers through the glass.

3. Put the lid on one of the jars. Turn the jars so that their tops face away from the sun. Then read the temperatures in both jars and write them down in your notebook.

4. Watch the jars. Record the air temperature every minute. When one thermometer gets close to the top of the scale, take the jars out of the sun and remove the lid. Otherwise, the thermometer could break.

SAFETY TIP WEAR YOUR OVEN MITTS WHEN HANDLING HOT JARS OR LIDS.

5. Look at the air temperatures you've recorded. Which jar got hotter than the other? Why do you think it did? How much hotter did it get? How long did it take?

What's going on?

The jar with the lid on traps heat rays inside the jar. Light rays easily pass through the glass into the jar, but heat rays can't easily pass through the glass and get out.

   The layer of gases building up around the Earth acts much as glass does. The gases allow the light in but prevent the heat from leaving. Carbon dioxide is the main gas causing the problem. Trees could help remove the carbon dioxide from the air, but we're cutting down too many forests.

Reach for the Sun

Plants need sunlight to grow and make food. How hard will a plant work to find the light? You might be amazed!

What you need

- A large cardboard box with dividers and a lid (get one at a grocery store or pharmacy)
- Scissors
- Garden soil
- A small flower pot
- 4 dried beans
- Strong, opaque tape (for example, electrical tape)

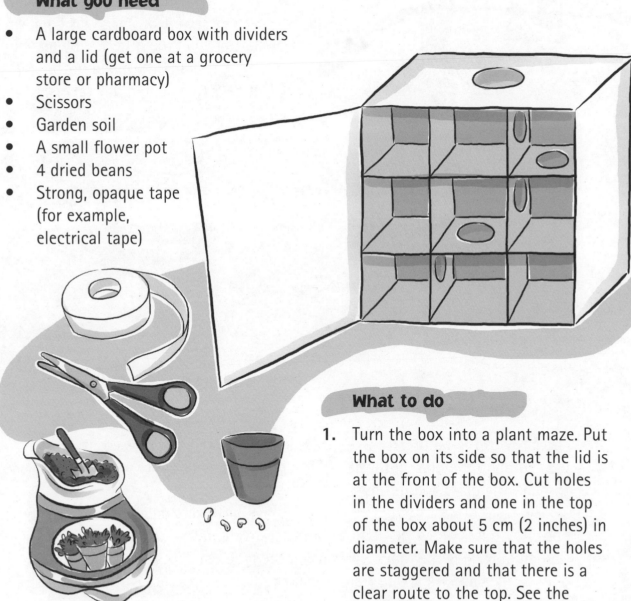

What to do

1. Turn the box into a plant maze. Put the box on its side so that the lid is at the front of the box. Cut holes in the dividers and one in the top of the box about 5 cm (2 inches) in diameter. Make sure that the holes are staggered and that there is a clear route to the top. See the picture for ideas.

86

2. Put garden soil in the pot and plant the beans. Water the soil lightly. Put the pot in a bottom corner of the box.

3. Close the lid and seal it with tape. You want to keep all light from entering the box except through the top hole.

4. Every 2 or 3 days, open the box to water the plant. When you've finished, reseal the box. Continue doing this for about 2 weeks.

5. What begins to happen in a few days? How far does your plant get in its journey to the light?

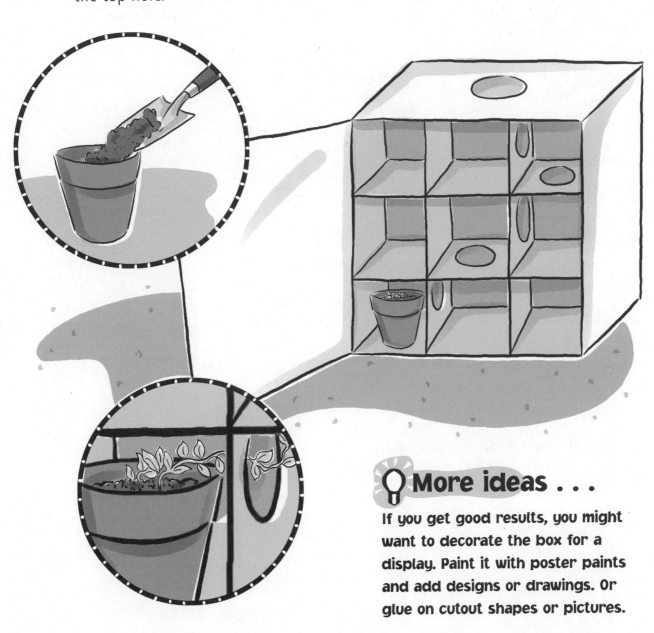

💡 More ideas . . .

If you get good results, you might want to decorate the box for a display. Paint it with poster paints and add designs or drawings. Or glue on cutout shapes or pictures.

Big Wheels

People have used water power for thousands of years. Water once turned wheels on machines for grinding grain or sawing wood. Build this old-fashioned water wheel and see if you can make it do some work.

What you need

- Scissors
- A large tinfoil pie plate
- A ruler
- A pencil
- Tape
- A piece of string about 50 cm (20 inches) long
- A small, light toy (for example, a plastic animal or toy car)

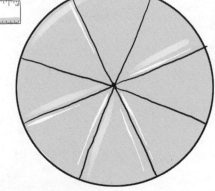

What to do

1. Cut the bottom out of the pie plate.

2. Find the center of the plate, or ask an adult to help. Use your ruler and pencil to draw lines through the center, dividing the circle into 8 equal sections.

3. Cut along the lines, stopping about 2 cm (³/₄ inch) from the center.

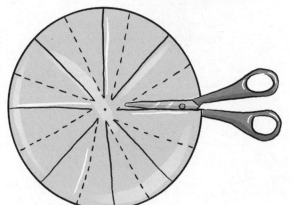

4. With your ruler, join the top of each cut to the middle of that section. Fold the edges back along the ruler to make blades, as shown in the picture.

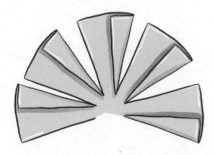

5. Punch a small hole in the center of the plate and push the pencil halfway through. Tape the pencil in place.

6. Turn on a faucet and let the water run slowly. (You might want some help here.) Hold the ends of the pencil lightly between your fingers. Now place your wheel under the stream of water so that the water hits the blades. The wheel should turn evenly. Try the wheel under a stronger stream. What happens?

7. Tie one end of the string to the pencil and attach the toy to the other end. Hold the wheel under the water stream again. Does the toy lift? If not, try a lighter object.

What's going on?

Your water wheel lifted the toy because water turned the wheel by falling on it from a height. Water at a high level has potential (stored) energy. Some of it changes to kinetic (moving) energy when it falls. Then, when the wheel turns, the energy changes again to mechanical energy, the kind that moves wheels, pulleys, and other machines.

Today, falling water in waterfalls mostly turns wheels to generate electricity. This hydroelectric power ("hydro" means "water") is renewable, because rain keeps refilling rivers and waterfalls. And unlike fossil fuels, water doesn't release carbon dioxide into the air. But waterpower has other environmental costs. Often waterfalls have to be created by building huge dams. Building these dams destroys large areas of land and the animals and plants in them.

And Now for a Commercial Message

Most commercials say, "Buy more." Why not create one that says, "Don't buy so much"? If we buy less stuff, we'll produce less waste and pollution and save more energy

What you need

- Scrap paper and a pencil
- A meter stick
- Stiff paper or cardboard
- Markers or crayons
- Drawing paper
- Tape
- Scissors
- A large cardboard carton
- A wooden dowel (about 1.2 m/4 feet long) or an old broom handle, to be cut into 2 dowels.

What to do

1. This is a group activity, so get some friends together. Brainstorm ideas for your commercial. You might want to study a few TV commercials to see what they do to sell the message.

2. When you have your story worked out, make a rough storyboard.

Draw 8 boxes on 1 or 2 sheets of scrap paper to represent TV screens. Roughly sketch the main scenes of your ad. Number the scenes.

3. Now write a rough script—what the characters and announcer say. If you're using music, write down the title of the song and when it starts and stops. Number the speeches to match the scenes. When you're happy with your script, make a cue card for each scene by printing the script for that scene in big letters on a sheet of stiff paper or cardboard.

4. Draw and color each scene on a full sheet of paper. Draw with the long sides at the top and bottom. Then tape the sheets together in order vertically. Add a blank sheet at each end. If you like, use black construction paper for the end pieces.

5. Cut out a rectangular shape in the front of the cardboard carton to represent the screen. Make the hole about 2 cm ($^3/_4$ inch) smaller all the way around than your pictures. Draw a few buttons on the side or along the bottom of the hole.

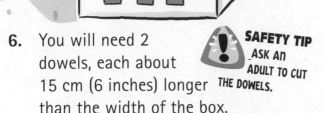

6. You will need 2 dowels, each about 15 cm (6 inches) longer than the width of the box.

SAFETY TIP
ASK AN ADULT TO CUT THE DOWELS.

7. Cut 2 holes on each side of the box, 1 at the top and 1 at the bottom, as shown in the picture. Put them about 3 cm (1 inch) from the front edges. Make the holes big enough to hold the dowels a bit loosely; the dowels should turn easily. Push the dowels into the holes.

8. Working through the open back of the box, securely tape the bottom edge of your last blank page to the bottom dowel. Turn the dowel to roll all the drawings firmly around it. Tape the top edge of the first blank page to the top dowel. Turn your dowels to pull the paper flat.

9. One person rolls the scenes by turning the top dowel. Another person holds the cue cards for the actors. And another handles the music. Practice a few times and then perform your commercial for an audience.

💡 More ideas . . .

You might prefer to act out your commercial using homemade costumes and props. If you have a video camera, you could even tape the performance and run it on TV.

5 Our Fine Feathered (and Leafy) Friends

If you were describing your school to someone, you could talk just about the other kids, the teachers, or the subjects you like or don't like so much. You could talk just about your classroom, the gym, or the cafeteria. But to give a complete picture of your school, you'd have to bring in all those things and say how they are related.

It's the same in the bigger world. It would be great if we knew all about the millions of species, or kinds, of plants and animals and how each one is connected to everything else. But we only have details about a tiny fraction of those plants and animals thought to exist. Yet we are killing them off at an incredible rate—some scientists estimate at an average of about six species per hour. And many more are in danger of extinction.

We kill or damage other animals and plants in many ways. We kill them directly for food, sport, and other uses. And we kill them indirectly by building cities, factories, and dams over their habitats and by polluting lakes and oceans full of water life. When we clear-cut a forest, we destroy a complex ecosystem in which the trees cleaned the air, trapped

flood waters, and made a home for thousands of species of wildlife. And that forest might have been part of a larger ecosystem that included a nearby river where salmon spawned.

We need our animal and plant relatives for more than the food, wood, cloth, medicines, and many other gifts they bring us. They are related to us through evolution, and they give us pleasure and inspiration. And they've been our companions for hundreds of thousands of years on our journey through the cosmos. We don't know all the reasons we need them, but we don't want to find out what those reasons are when it's too late.

The best way to learn about the natural world is to explore it. Get out into the fields, into the woods, or on the seashore as much as you can. Quietly look around. Wait, because nature needs time to show itself to you. Watch the birds sail through the clouds. Listen. Hear the buzz of insects and the whistle of the wind through the trees. Breathe deeply and smell the perfume of flowers and the soil. Close your eyes and feel the breeze on your skin and the sun's rays on your face. You belong here because it's your home, too.

Remember these things as you do the following activities. Some of them will take you out into nature, so make the most of your time there. You'll be learning some fascinating things about your animal and plant kin. You'll explore how they relate to their environments, to the Earth, and to you. And you'll find lots of ideas for helping take care of the home we all share.

Autumn Bug Hunt

There's more to fall than stomping through piles of fallen leaves, fun as that is. It's also a perfect time to take a good look at some of the tiny creatures who share your neighborhood.

What you need

- A pooter (see page 95)
- A large plastic container (for a scoop)
- Fallen leaves
- A large garbage bag
- A white cotton sheet or large piece of plain, light-colored paper
- A magnifying glass
- A small spoon
- A small yogurt container
- Drawing materials

What to do

1. First, make your pooter.

2. Collect a few scoops of fallen leaves and put them in the garbage bag. Scoop right down to the soil or grass level, where bugs are most likely to be.

3. Lay the sheet or paper on a worktable or the floor. Spread the leaves out over the sheet.

To make a pooter

- Get a small, clear jar with lid, 2 fat, flexible straws, some plasticine, a small piece of nylon stocking, and some tape.

- With a nail and hammer, punch 2 holes in the lid large enough for the straws to fit into.

SAFETY TIP
YOU MIGHT WANT AN ADULT'S HELP WITH THE HAMMER AND NAIL.

- Stick the straws into the lid and seal the spaces around them with plasticine. For your mouthpiece, cut the outside end of one straw down to about 6 cm (2³⁄₈ inches); tape the nylon piece over the other end of the straw. Screw the lid firmly onto the jar.
- To collect an insect, hold the long straw over it while you suck gently through the other straw. The insect will be drawn into the jar.

4. Examine the leaves carefully with your magnifying glass. When you find an insect, gently spoon it into the yogurt container. For very small insects, use your pooter.

5. When you have several insects, study them with your magnifying glass. Make detailed drawings of them. How many legs do they have? How are their bodies subdivided? Can you see any hairs? Look at the antennae on their heads, their mouth parts, and their color patterns.

6. If you have a book about the insects of your region, try to identify your bugs. Write their names under the drawings. Add an important fact about each.

7. When you have finished, return the insects and leaves to where you found them.

💡 More ideas . . .

- **Make a display of your drawings, arranging them in any groupings you like—for example, by size, color, or type of insect.**

- **Research your most interesting insect and write a description of its life and habits.**

Make Your Own Paper

Can you imagine a world without paper—no books, magazines, drawing paper, or newspapers? Paper is made with fibers from trees. We can save a lot of trees from being cut down by recycling used paper. Here's a simple way to make your own recycled paper. You could use it for greeting cards, drawings, or letters. Or make the sheets half-size and hand out your own business cards!

What you need

- A stack of old newspapers
- A large bowl
- 500 mL (2 cups) warm water
- 15 mL (1 tablespoon) dishwashing liquid
- An eggbeater, electric mixer, or blender
- A piece of wire window screening, about 10 cm x 12 cm (4 inches x 5 inches)
- A rolling pin
- Optional: grated carrot or other vegetable, food coloring, leaves

What to do

1. Cover a flat work surface with lots of newspaper—paper making can get messy.

2. Tear 1 sheet of newspaper into tiny bits and put them in the bowl. (This will make 2 or 3 sheets of paper.)

3. Add the water and dishwashing liquid and stir. Let the mixture soak until it's very soft—at least 2 hours.

SAFETY TIP
ASK FOR PERMISSION BEFORE USING A MIXER OR BLENDER.

4. Beat the mixture into a mush using an eggbeater, an electric mixer, or a blender.

5. Slide the screen into the bowl and lift out a thin layer of pulp. Smooth the pulp with your fingers so that there are no holes. Gently shake the screen to get rid of extra water.

6. Lay the screen in the middle of a whole section of newspaper. Close the section and flip it over so that the screen ends up on top of the pulp. Don't forget to do this step!

7. Roll the paper with a rolling pin to flatten it and squeeze out water. Press hard with your hands on the roller. Open the paper and carefully peel off the screen. Close the newspaper and roll again.

8. Tear off the top wet sheet and replace it with dry newspaper. Put a weight such as a large book on top. (If the weight can be damaged by water, put some plastic bags under it.) Let the paper dry for at least 24 hours. When it's dry, carefully peel off the bottom newspaper.

💡 More ideas . . .

- **To make colored paper, add a few drops of food coloring at step 3.**

- **For a pretty speckled pattern, stir into the mush 2 mL (1/2 teaspoon) of grated carrot or chopped parsely at step 4. For glam, add glitter!**

- **Press leaf patterns into your paper. After removing the screen, lay 1 or more leaves, rib-side down, on the pulp and roll flat.**

Hunting Tag

The animal world is made up of carnivores (meat eaters, such as wildcats), herbivores (plant eaters, such as deer), and omnivores (food combiners, such as robins, which eat both plants and animals). Pretend you are an animal in the wild. You have to hunt for all your food. How long can you survive?

What you need

- A group of friends (these instructions are for 8, but any number can play)
- A large open area such as a park, school yard, or big backyard
- Red, green, yellow, and blue construction paper
- Scissors
- A ruler
- String or cord
- Tape

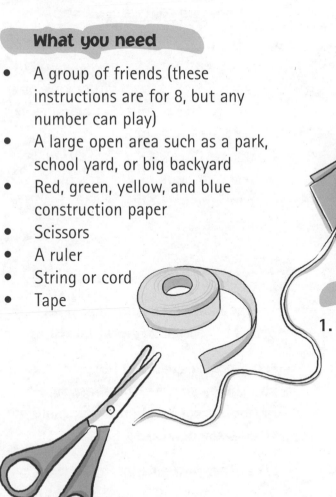

What to do

1. Before the game, make 8 identification cards out of construction paper. Cut 2 cards, each about 5 cm x 10 cm (2 inches x 4 inches), out of each color of paper. Then cut 8 pieces of string, each about 60 cm (2 feet) long. Tape the ends of the strings to the backs of the cards.

2. At the beginning of each round, players close their eyes and draw cards to determine which creature they will be: a meat eater (red), plant eater (blue), food combiner (yellow), or plant (green). They wear their ID cards around their necks.

3. Players spread out. On a signal, they begin to hunt for food and hide from predators. If a prey is tagged, he or she has been eaten and is out of the round. Animals can hunt their particular food or hide, but plants can only hide.

4. The last plant or animal to survive is the winner of the round. He or she gets 1 point.

5. In one round, tell players the habitat has been hit by a disaster—drought, fire, disease, deforestation, or unlimited hunting by humans. Have one player (no ID card) represent the threat. This player cannot be hunted but can tag any other player. How long does this round last and who is the winner?

6. Play at least 10 rounds. The player with the most points at the end of the game is declared Wizard of the Wild.

What's going on?

The food habits of animals in the wild tend to keep populations in balance. But severe threats can quickly destroy that balance.

Plant a Tree

Planting a tree is one of the best things you can do for the environment. Trees are nature's air conditioners—they help cool and clean the air. They also provide homes for wildlife and hold water in the ground. You'll want your friends, family, or class to help with this one.

What you need

- A young tree (seedling)
- A shovel
- Water
- Mulch (dry leaves, pine needles, or wood chips)

What to do

1. Decide where you want to plant your tree and ask permission from the owner or manager of the land. That could be the city council if you want to plant on city land, the principal of your school if you choose the school yard, or your parents if you're planting in your backyard (which might be a good place to start).

2. Check with local environmental organizations to see if there are any programs in your area that give away trees for planting. If not,

get a tree from a nursery or garden center. Ask a worker there to help you choose a tree that will grow well in your area. Ask what kind of soil and location is best for your tree, how much sun it needs, and whether there is any other information you should have.

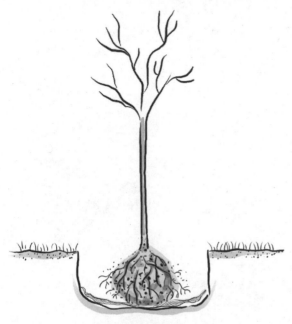

3. Dig a hole as deep as the tree's root ball and twice as wide. If the soil around the hole is really hard, loosen it up a bit with the shovel.

4. If the tree is in a container, remove the container from the root ball. Carefully spread out the roots.

5. If the roots are tied up in burlap, remove the rope. You can leave the burlap lying at the bottom of the hole, however. Burlap is made from plants, so it will rot away over time.

6. Place the tree in the hole. Fill the hole with soil and tramp it down well. Make sure the level of the soil comes up to the top of the root ball.

7. Make a little ridge of soil or grass clumps around the edge of the hole to hold in water. Then give your tree a good soaking—about 10 L (10 quarts) of water. You'll have to keep on watering it every week (unless it rains or snows) for a whole year.

8. Pile mulch around the trunk of the tree but not touching it.

9. This is *your* tree. Watch it grow along with you.

More ideas . . .

- Many community groups and schools organize tree-planting days as part of larger projects. Get some friends together and volunteer. Or, organize your own community project. Get the event rolling by inviting community groups such as the Boy Scouts or Girl Guides to help.

- Raise money to buy your trees. You could hold a bake sale, sell tickets for a raffle (ask local businesses to donate prizes), or organize a car wash at a local mall parking lot or gas station.

Animal Yoga

Want to get in touch with your inner animal? These ancient yoga stretches will help you feel strong, relaxed, and calm. Wear stretchy or loose clothing and warm up by running on the spot for a couple of minutes before you start. Hold a position for several seconds—whatever feels right.

FROG ON A LILY PAD

Sit very tall with your knees bent and the soles of your feet together. Hold your feet and pull them in as close as you can. Imagine your spine getting longer. Press your thighs down. Hold, then relax.

RISING COBRA

Lie on your stomach with your elbows bent and hands beside your shoulders. Slowly push up until your arms are straight. Keep your hips on the floor. Hold, then relax back down.

CAT STRETCH

SAFETY TIP NEVER FORCE A STRETCH UNTIL IT HURTS. MOVE SLOWLY AND SMOOTHLY AND TAKE SLOW, DEEP BREATHS.

Kneel on all fours with your back flat. Tuck your tailbone in. Push your back up high as you lower your head and look between your knees. Hold, then relax.

MONKEY WALK

Walk around on all fours, keeping your legs as straight as you can. Stop and slowly curl up to a standing position, letting your head come up last.

KNEELING CAMEL

Kneel with your right hand on your right heel and left hand on your left heel. Bend your head back and push your chest up. Hold, then stretch one arm up as if you were grabbing a rope. Pull yourself up and relax. Repeat, stretching the other arm up.

STORK IN THE WATER

Stand straight with feet together and arms at your sides. Bend your right leg to the side and put your foot on the inside of your left thigh as high as you can. When you have your balance, slowly raise your arms over your head and stretch high. Hold and then relax your leg and arms down. Repeat with the other leg.

DOZING JELLYFISH

Lie flat on your back with your arms and legs comfortably spread out. Close your eyes and relax completely, as if your bones were made of jelly. Rest there, breathing slowly and softly, for as long as you like.

Well Rooted

Plants are essential to the health of every ecosystem. Their leaves clean the air, their branches shelter birds and insects, and their roots dig deep into the soil. Soil helps the plant by giving it nutrients and moisture, but the plant helps the soil just as much. In this experiment, you'll see one important thing plant roots do to keep the soil healthy.

What you need

- Some seeds (for example, radish, mustard, or bean seeds)
- A large clear jar
- Some rich garden soil
- A paper cup

What to do

1. Put 5 seeds into the jar. Fill the jar halfway with water. Leave it for about 3 days. The seeds should start to sprout.

2. Fill the cup about three-quarters full of soil. Plant 3 seedlings (sprouted seeds) in the cup. Pick the seedlings that look healthiest. Push them about 2 cm (³/4 inch) into the soil.

3. Water your plant lightly and put it in a sunny spot for about 2 weeks. Water the plant every day to keep the soil just moist.

4. After 2 weeks, you should have a leafy plant. Carefully peel away the paper cup from the soil. What are the roots doing and what do they look like? What does the soil look like? Does it fall off the roots?

What's happening?

If you've ever weeded dandelions in a garden, you'll know how strong roots can be. Roots hold the plant firmly in the ground, and they hold the soil together, too. How do you think this helps the soil?

Diary of a Tree

If you have a pet, you know how much you learn about dogs or cats or fish by living with one and watching and playing with it. The same is true of trees. A great way to learn about trees is to adopt a special tree for a season or a year.

What you need

- A notebook and pen or pencil
- A tape measure
- A magnifying glass
- Art materials for making drawings, rubbings, and prints
- Optional: a camera

What to do

1. Pick out a tree. It shouldn't be too far from your home, since you'll be visiting it often. Some things to think about: A deciduous tree (one that sheds its leaves in the fall) will go through more big changes than an evergreen. And a large, healthy tree is likely to have a lot happening in it.

2. Find out what kind of tree it is and then do some research. You can find information in library books and on the Internet. Write in your notebook anything that interests you about the tree—for example, its scientific name, the places where it grows (on hills or in valleys, in wet or dry places), its life cycle, the animals that depend on it for food or homes, and so on.

3. On your first visit, study the tree and write a description of it. Measure the circumference of the trunk with a tape measure. Look closely at the bark with a magnifying glass and draw a picture of its patterns, or take a rubbing (see page 114). Do you see any animals in the tree? Are there nuts or berries forming? Close your eyes and take a deep breath. What do you smell? What do you hear?

4. In spring, summer, and fall, take a leaf home. Press it (see page 114) and tape it into your book. If the tree has flowers, you could press one and add it. If you've chosen a fruit tree, make a fruit print (see page 115) and add that to your book.

5. Set aside separate sections in your book for any interesting animals that come to your tree. If birds nest in it, find out what they are and follow what happens over the summer. You might want to do some research on them, too. Be careful not to frighten nesting birds. Move slowly and quietly and don't get too close.

6. Visit your tree once a week for a season or a year, if possible. Each time write down the date and what you observe. If you have a camera, you could take pictures of the tree in different seasons.

♀ More ideas . . .

- Give your tree a name. Write a diary entry from the point of view of the tree.

- Maybe you'll want to study other kinds of trees to see how they differ from your first one.

Sign an Earth Message

Talking is only one way to express your ideas. You can also sing, dance, draw a picture—or sign.

What you need

- Your 2 hands
- Some imagination

What to do

Practice signing these words with a friend. Then sign a message or poem.

wish

save – tap fingers

home – 2 touches

my, mine

Earth – wiggle fingers back and forth

happy – brush hand up off chest

you

water – tap chin

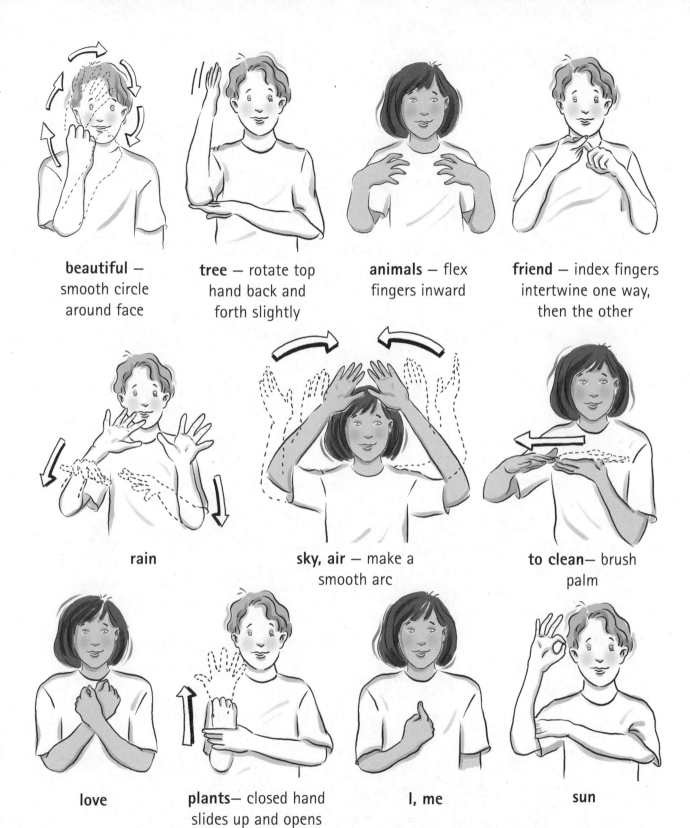

beautiful — smooth circle around face

tree — rotate top hand back and forth slightly

animals — flex fingers inward

friend — index fingers intertwine one way, then the other

rain

sky, air — make a smooth arc

to clean — brush palm

love

plants — closed hand slides up and opens

I, me

sun

No Place Like Home

Animals live in habitats as different as hot, dry deserts, tropical rain forests, and the bottom of oceans. But no animal can thrive everywhere. Most prefer certain kinds of habitats. Find out what some animals in your environment like in the place they call home.

What you need

- A toilet paper roll
- Scissors
- A pencil
- 2 roomy boxes the same size (for example, shoeboxes), with lids
- Masking tape
- Extra cardboard
- A few small animals common in your area (for example, ants, worms, snails)
- Leaves (from where you found the animals) and other food
- Plastic wrap
- A hot-water bottle

What to do

1. Cut a door flap in the side of the toilet paper roll (see the picture). Punch a few air holes in the box lids.

2. Trace around the end of the toilet paper roll on the side and near the bottom of each box. Cut a hole in each box and fit the tube into the two holes. Tape it into place. This will be a "hall" joining the 2 boxes.

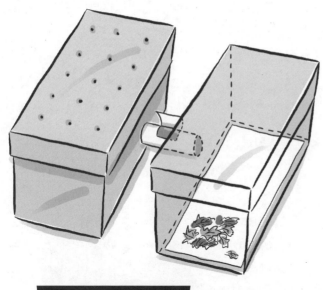

LIGHT OR DARK?

Remove the animals, food, and cardboard floors and repeat the experiment. This time, take off the lid of one box and cover it with plastic wrap. Add food and check the next day. Which room are your animals in now?

WARM OR COOL?

Repeat the experiment, using lids on both boxes, with one box sitting on a hot-water bottle. Refill the bottle when the water cools so that the box stays very warm. Check in about 4 hours.

HUMID OR DRY?

1. Cut a piece of cardboard to fit the bottom of each box. Wet 1 piece and keep the other dry. Put them in the boxes as floors.

2. Add some food (for example, shredded leaves) to each box.

3. Put the animals into their new habitat through the door flap. Put on the lids and tape the flap shut. After 2 days, which room are your animals living in?

When you are finished, put the animals back where you found them. According to your tests, what 3 features do your animals want in their habitat?

Survivors

In this board game, each player is in charge of three animal species on the endangered list. Can you save your animals from extinction?

What you need

- A sheet of white poster board (50 cm x 72 cm/20 inches x 28 inches)
- Scissors
- A meter stick (or yardstick)
- A pencil, a pushpin, and a piece of string about 60 cm (2 feet) long
- Markers (black, green, blue)
- 12 bottle caps
- Construction paper (brown, tan, orange, yellow)
- White glue
- A die (1 of a pair of dice)

To make the game

1. Cut off 1 end of the poster board to make a square 50 cm (20 inches) on each side. Measure and outline a 5-cm (2-inch) border around the edges.

2. Join the corners with light, diagonal pencil lines. Where they cross is the center of the board. Use the string, pushpin, and pencil to draw a series of circles about 3 cm (1¼ inches) apart, as shown in the picture. Color the circles, alternating green and blue. Decorate the border.

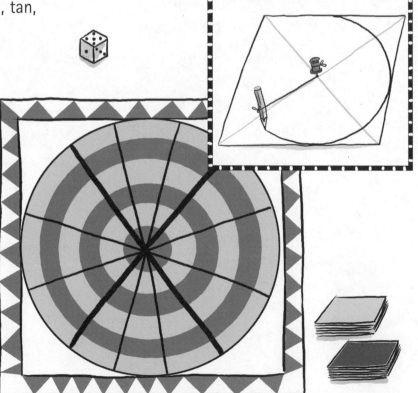

3. Choose 12 endangered animal species (check out library books or Web sites—for example, look at the World Wildlife Fund at http://www.worldwildlife.org/). Make labels for the bottle caps from the brown, tan, orange, and yellow construction paper—3 in each color. Write the names of the 12 species (you can use the short forms) on the labels and glue them to the bottle caps. These are your markers.

4. From the green and blue construction paper, cut out and mark cards as follows:

Green cards

No. of cards

3	Habitat Destroyed—extinct (out of the game)
2	Glacier Melt—extinct (out of the game)
3	Pollution—move back 3 spaces
4	Drought—move back 3 spaces
4	Fire—miss next turn
2	Dam Built—move back 2 spaces
2	Hurricane—move back 2 spaces
2	Flood—move back 2 spaces
2	Building Project Cancelled—stay put
4	Hunting Laws—advance 2 spaces
3	Conservation Area—advance 2 spaces
4	Sunshine—advance 1 space
4	Rainfall—advance 2 spaces

Blue cards

No. of cards

15	Food
15	Famine

To play the game

1. Shuffle each pile of cards well. Give each player a set of 3 endangered-animal markers. Players roll the die in turn. Players must roll a 6 to put each of their animals at the center circle to be born.

2. Players roll the die in turn and move the number of spaces they roll. They pick up the top card of the color they land on and follow the instructions. If they get a blue card, they keep it. Players must move one animal at a time.

3. Players must have a blue Food card set aside when an animal reaches the edge of the board. But if they also have a Famine card, it cancels out the Food card and both cards must be shuffled back into the blue pile. If they don't have a Food card, they must wait until they collect one to save their animal.

4. The game continues until only one player is left. The player who gets the most species off the board alive has saved them from extinction and wins the game.

Press, Rub, Print

Plants may die in the fall, but you can preserve some of their beauty by pressing them or making rubbings and prints. You can use any of these techniques to make greeting cards or wrapping paper or to decorate a letter. Or you can tape them into your nature notebook. A collection of plants native to your area could be put into a book with a label telling where and when each was found.

A PRESSING ENGAGEMENT

What you need: Leaves, flowers, or grasses; clean paper; heavy books

Place a leaf, flower, or grass on a piece of paper and cover with a second sheet of paper. Put some heavy books on top and leave the pile for about 3 weeks.

RUBBINGS THE RIGHT WAY

What you need: Masking tape, white paper, wax crayons

1. Make bark rubbings on dry days. Find a tree that has interesting markings on its bark. Tape a piece of paper to the bark. Break off a small piece of crayon and tear off the paper around it. Rub the side of the crayon firmly up and down on the bark until the pattern appears on the paper taped to the tree. Be careful not to tear the paper.

2. To make a leaf rubbing, lay a leaf on a flat surface, vein-side up. Put a piece of paper over it. Rub a crayon evenly across the leaf until you get a clear outline.

PRINTS CHARMING

What you need: Pressed leaves, poster paints, white or colored paper, paintbrush, knife, tinfoil pie plate

1. To make a leaf print, paint the veined side of a leaf with your brush. Gently press the leaf on a piece of paper. When the paint is dry, you can paint other leaves different colors and make patterns.

2. Firm fruits and vegetables with interesting insides (for example, pears, apples, oranges, green peppers) make beautiful prints, too. Cut oranges in half across the center and the other fruits or vegetables lengthwise. Pour some paint into the pie plate and tip it around to cover the bottom. Dip the fruit or vegetable into the paint. Press the fruit or vegetable straight down onto the paper and then lift it straight up. To get a clear print, be careful not to move the fruit or vegetable while it's on the paper. This method also works well for meadow grasses and mushrooms (print the underside of the cap).

Grade Your Home for Greenness

We can help the environment a lot right in our own homes. So how are you doing? Take a tour and answer this "green home" quiz.

1. If possible, do you recycle rather than throw these away? (1 point each)

   a) Cans ____
   b) Newspapers ____
   c) Other kinds of paper ____
   d) Cardboard ____
   e) Glass bottles ____
   f) Old clothes ____
   g) Plastic bags ____
   h) Plastic bottles ____
   i) Used motor oil from the car ____
   j) Anything else?

   _____

2. Do you make compost out of (a) kitchen waste and (b) yard waste? (5 points each)

3. Do you reuse old containers (plastic tubs, cans, boxes, jars, and so on) for other things? List uses (2 points each, up to 10 points or 5 uses):

   _____
   _____
   _____
   _____
   _____

4. Do you take dangerous garbage to a Hazardous Waste Depot? (10 points)_____

   Add a bonus point if you can pick out the only one of the following items that is *not* hazardous: paint, turpentine, vinegar, car battery acid, drain cleaner, medicines, lighter fluid, pesticides, needles, aerosol spray cans. _____

5. Do you turn out lights when leaving a room? _____

6. In winter, do you keep the house temperature coolish during the day (you can wear a sweater) and even cooler at night? (10 points)_____

7. In summer, do you water lawns not more than once or twice a week? (10 points) _____

8. Do you use safer, homemade alternatives or buy "green" products for the following? (2 points each)

   a) Window cleaner _____
   b) Laundry detergent _____
   c) Pesticides and weed killers

   _____
   d) Floor cleaners _____
   e) Anything else? _____

9. Do you use rags (worn-out diapers and dish towels are good choices) instead of paper towels or disposable cloths for cleaning? (10 points) _____

10. Add any green habit your family has that is not on the list. (For example, walking, biking, or taking public transportation instead of traveling by car, or choosing products with the least packaging or the most environmentally friendly packaging.) (10 points)

   _____

11. Now *subtract* 1 point for every leaky tap you find. Minus _____

12. Count how many electric appliances you have in the house. You might get a shock! (That pun was on purpose.) Count each light bulb and don't forget small items such as toothbrushes and can openers. Discuss with your family whether you are using any appliances you could do without. Subtract 1 point for each of those. Minus_____

Add (and subtract) the points to get your home's Green Grade: _____

80 to 100	Bright green like a summer leaf
60 to 79	Yellow-green like a spring leaf
40 to 59	Pale yellow and ready to fall
Under 40	You're on the ground!

4. Vinegar

Glossary

atmosphere The air surrounding the Earth.

atom The smallest particle of matter.

bacteria Creatures so small that you can only see them with a microscope; often called germs. Most kinds of bacteria are helpful, and a few are harmful.

biodegradable Able to be broken down by bacteria or other living organisms.

biodiversity The variety of plants, animals, and ecosystems in the world.

carnivore A meat-eating animal, such as a leopard, or a plant that traps and digests insects.

chlorophyll The green-colored chemicals found in the leaves of green plants. They carry out photosynthesis, converting sunlight to chemical energy.

condensation The change from a gas to a liquid, usually caused by a drop in the temperature of the gas. For example, water vapor (a gas) in the air condenses into drops of water (a liquid) when it hits the outside of a glass of iced lemonade.

decomposer An organism that feeds on dead plants and animals by breaking them down into nutrients. Decomposers (such as earthworms, bacteria, and fungi) return these nutrients to the soil, water, or bodies of animals who eat them.

deforestation The cutting down or burning of the trees in a forest to leave cleared land.

ecology The study of the relationships between organisms and their environment.

ecosystem A community of animals and plants and their relationships with each other and their environment.

environment The living things, climate, soil, air, and other factors that surround an organism.

erosion The wearing down of soil, rock, or other solid substances by wind, rain, ice, and other forces.

evaporation	The change from a liquid to a gas, usually caused by a rise in temperature. For example, water (a liquid) changes into water vapor, or steam (a gas), when it is boiled.
filtering	Removing solid particles from a liquid or gas by passing it through a filter, such as stones, charcoal, or special paper.
fossil	The remains or impression of an ancient plant or animal preserved in rock.
fungus	An organism that is similar to a plant but does not have chlorophyll and reproduces by means of spores rather than seeds. Mushrooms, rust, and mold are examples of fungi (plural of *fungus*).
geotropic	Tending to grow or turn toward the Earth. Plant roots, for instance, are geotropic. "Geo" is Greek for "Earth."
habitat	The place where an animal or plant naturally lives or grows.
hazardous	Dangerous.
heliotropic	Tending to grow or turn toward the sun. For example, flowers are heliotropic. Helios was the Greek god of the sun.
herbivore	An animal that eats only plants—for example, deer and hippopotamuses.
humus	The organic part of soil, made of partly rotted plant and animal matter.
irrigation	A system that puts water into dry land by using pipes, ditches, or streams.
kinetic energy	Energy relating to movement.
landfill	An underground garbage dump. A hole is dug in the ground and usually lined with plastic or clay. Garbage is dumped into the hole, pressed flat by bulldozers, and covered by soil. When it is full, the landfill is closed.
mass	The amount of matter that an object contains and that causes it to have weight.
mechanical energy	Energy produced by machines such as wheels, pulleys, and gears.
microscopic	Very small; can only be seen by looking through a microscope.
molecule	A group of atoms. All matter is made up of molecules. Each substance has a different kind of molecule. For example, water molecules are different from salt molecules.

nonrenewable   Not able to be made or renewed—for example, a resource or form of energy, such as coal, oil, and gas, that can be used up because there is only a certain amount of it in the world.

omnivore   An animal that eats both plants and animals—for example, bears and raccoons.

organic   Coming from plants or animals.

organism   A living plant or animal.

photosynthesis   The process by which green plants take in carbon dioxide and water vapor from the air and, using sunlight and chlorophyll (the leaves' green coloring material), make food and give off oxygen.

potential energy   Stored energy. Water at a height has potential energy, some of which will be released when it falls.

pressure   Force pressing against one object by another object.

recycle   To crush, melt down, or otherwise change something that has already been used to make a new item instead of throwing the used item away. For example, glass bottles can be crushed and made into pavement, and old paper can be used to make more paper.

renewable   Able to be regrown or replaced over and over. For example, trees, water, gases such as methane, and sunshine are all renewable sources of energy.

solar   Having to do with the sun.

species   A group of plants or animals that share certain characteristics and can reproduce with each other. The domestic dog and the African camel are examples of species.

stoma   A microscopic pore in the surface of leaves and stems through which gases are released and taken in. Plural is *stomata*.

transpiration   The release of water vapor by plants.

vacuum   A space that has had all the air removed from it. A partial vacuum is a space that has some of the air removed.

Index

Acknowledgments

The authors consulted many sources in putting together this book and especially acknowledge the following: Susan V. Bosak with Douglas A. Bosak and Brian A. Puppa, *Science Is...*, 2nd ed. (Richmond Hill, Ont.: Scholastic Canada, and Markham, Ont.: The Communication Project, 1991); *The Animal Kingdom: Science Activities for the Study of Animals* and *Soil: Science Activities for the Study of the Earth* (Vancouver: Mindscape Publishing Co., 1989); David Suzuki with Barbara Hehner, *Looking at Plants* and *Looking at the Environment*, Stoddart Young Readers series (Toronto: Stoddart, 1985 and 1989); and Brenda Walpole, *Exploring Nature Funstation* (Los Angeles: Price Stern Sloan, 1995, produced by Design Eye Holdings).

Thanks also to Chuck Heath of Ridgeway Elementary School in North Vancouver, B.C., and Gordon Li of Marlborough School in Burnaby, B.C., for reviewing the manuscript; the students at Marlborough School who tried out some of the activities; Melanie Huddart, Jennifer Glossop, Janet McCutcheon, Marilyn Roy, Sharon Sterling, Karen Virag, and Farida Wahab for help and advice; Nancy Flight for her expert editing; Warren Clark and Jane Kurisu for making the book look good; and Tony Makepeace for hanging in.